Interpreting Empty Houses

Ana Ruiz, M.A.F.A.

Copyright 2006 by Ana Ruiz

No part of this book may be reproduced or transcribed in any form or by any means, electronic or mechanical, including photocopying or recording, or by any information storage and retrieval system without written permission from the author and publisher, except in the case of brief quotations embodied in critical reviews and articles. Requests and inquiries may be mailed to: American Federation of Astrologers, Inc., 6535 S. Rural Road, Tempe, AZ 85283.

First Printing: 2006

ISBN 10: 0-86690-569-3
ISBN 13: 978-0-86690-569-5

Cover Design: Jack Cipolla

Published by:
American Federation of Astrologers, Inc.
6535 S. Rural Road
Tempe, AZ 85283

Printed in the United States of America

Foreword

I wish to acknowledge and thank Rex E. Bills for his work, *The Rulership Book*, published by the American Federation of Astrologers. This has been an invaluable guide to me that no astrologer should be without. Also available through the American Federation of Astrologers is *Prediction Techniques Regarding Romance* by Ana Ruiz. Also by this author is *The Spirit of Ancient Egypt*, published by Algora Publishing.

I dedicate this to all the astrologers
of the past, present and future.

Contents

Introduction	vii
First House	1
Second House	35
Third House	45
Fourth House	57
Fifth House	71
Sixth House	83
Seventh House	97
Eighth House	111
Ninth House	123
Tenth House	135
Eleventh House	149
Twelfth House	163
Case Studies	177

Introduction

Houses void of planets are often overlooked, particularly by beginners in astrology. A little more effort is required on the part of the astute astrologer in interpreting empty houses but is well worth the effort in terms of understanding the chart and native as a whole. Empty houses however, may not exert as much influence or be as important to the native than houses that contain planets, yet they are nevertheless still active, interpretable and influential. For example, a seventh or house of marriage without any planets does not indicate the absence of marriage but rather that other areas of life are of more relevance and the native may or may not marry, depending on the aspects formed to this planetary ruler of this empty seventh house.

When a house in a natal chart contains a planet or planets, much information is derived about the conditions, tendencies, opportunities or challenges surrounding that area in question from the planet(s) therein. When a house is void of planets, much information can still be derived, but one has to look deeper. The planetary ruler of the sign found on this empty house becomes the key that unlocks the door of this house to awaiting information that is to be interpreted by the astrologer.

This planet is closely analyzed by house, sign and aspect(s) formed with other planets. The aspects involving the ruler of an empty house are of utmost importance in determining the nature of its influence, as it is a recipient of other planetary energies. Planets forming favorable aspects to a particular house ruler show promise and success in the area ruled by the houses involved in the aspect. Difficult aspects point out where challenges and obstacles are encountered in the area ruled by the houses involved in the aspect. The house placing of the ruler shows where these opportunities or challenges are available, encountered and experienced.

The planetary ruler of an empty house becomes its sole ruler or 'lord.' This planet becomes the secondary ruler if the house contains a planet as the latter exerts a much greater influence. If more than one planet is positioned in a house, the ruler of the sign on that house receives the least priority and therefore is weakest as it is overpowered by the planets therein that are much stronger. A planet within 5 degrees from a house cusp also influences the empty house that it is either approaching or departing.

When working only with the Sun through Pluto, there are always at least two empty houses in a chart as the 10 planets (including the luminaries, the Sun and Moon) are positioned throughout the 12 houses of the horoscope. Stelliums naturally increase the number of empty houses as they are grouped into specific houses leaving more than two vacant.

Houses

Additional factors need to be considered when analyzing the ruler of an empty house.

The strengths, elements and qualities of the house holding the ruler provides valuable insight. The first group is the qualities of the houses. The strongest houses are the angular or cardinal houses being the first, fourth, seventh and tenth. These correspond to the traditional cardinal signs, Aries, Cancer, Libra and Capricorn. These houses are positioned on the angles of the horoscope and exert the most influence. If few or no planets are found within these houses, enthusiasm, spark, assertiveness, ambition, initiative and drive may be deficient or lacking.

The next houses of lesser importance are called the succedent or fixed houses being the second, fifth, eighth and eleventh. These correspond to the traditional fixed signs, Taurus, Leo, Scorpio and Aquarius. Few or no planets in these houses indicate an individual who may lack permanence, determination, commitment and perseverance.

The weakest houses are called cadent or mutable houses being the third, sixth, ninth and twelfth. These correspond to the traditional mutable or common signs, Gemini, Virgo, Sagittarius and Pisces. Few or no planets in these houses indicate an individual who may lack flexibility, versatility and adaptability.

The next group to be analyzed is the elements of the houses. Like the signs, they are divided into fire, earth, air and water. The fire houses are the first, fifth and ninth, naturally ruled by the fire signs, Aries, Leo and Sagittarius. Few or no planets in these houses indicate a lack of enthusiasm, vitality, ambition, self-confidence, leadership potential and creativity. They are also known as the Houses of Life.

The earth houses are the second, sixth and tenth, naturally ruled by the earth signs, Taurus, Virgo and Capricorn. Few or no planets in these houses bring financial or professional insecurity or instability. Practicality, reliability and persistence may be lacking. They are also called the Houses of Substance or Wealth.

The air houses are the third, seventh and eleventh, naturally ruled by the air signs, Gemini, Libra and Aquarius. Few or no planets in these houses indicate that emotions tend to rule over reason. There can be a lack of sociability, intellectual creativity, or flexibility. They are also called the Houses of Relationships.

The water houses are the fourth, eighth and twelfth, naturally ruled by the water signs, Cancer, Scorpio and Pisces. Few or no planets in these houses indicate that reason tends to rule over emotions. Sensitivity, intuition and the ability to express feelings may be lacking. They are also called the Houses of Emotions or Endings.

A point that is imperative to mention is that if the Ascendant or Sun sign is found in a particular element or quality that is lacking within the chart, it adequately compensates for this deficit.

Planets

If the ruler of the house in question is retrograde, its delineation is slightly altered. Mercury in retrograde motion indicates a careful mentality that does not jump to conclusions or speak without first thinking. The native constantly rethinks ideas and decisions, therefore, decision-making can be slow and deliberate. Ideas and opinions are not expressed unless they are very well thought out. These influences are applied to the area of life or house holding and ruled by Mercury and are especially important if Mercury is the ruler of the Ascendant or Sun sign.

Venus in retrograde motion at birth indicates a possible limited or blocked manner of expressing or demonstrating affections and emotions. Criticism hurts deeply and feelings can be profound, but usually maintained deep within. These influences are applied to the area of life or house holding and ruled by Venus and are particularly important if Venus is the ruler of the Ascendant or Sun sign.

A retrograde Mars shows the tendency to go back and recheck actions and decisions until the native is satisfied. Energies are mainly directed inwards and much inner strength can be drawn upon when needed. However, assertiveness may be lacking. These influences are applied to the area of life or house holding and ruled by Mars and are of special significance if Mars is the ruler of the Ascendant or Sun sign.

When Jupiter is retrograde, there is much independence of thought. This individual cannot be swayed or converted to another's beliefs or ideologies. The need to cultivate optimism, spirituality, a sense of humor and an expansive mind is evident. These influences are applied to the area of life or house holding and ruled by Jupiter and are especially important if Jupiter rules the Ascendant or Sun sign.

Saturn in retrograde motion indicates that by accepting the restrictions and limitations this planet can bring, progress can eventually be realized. A sense of humor and self-confidence is especially important to cultivate as pessimism is likely. There are likely neglected responsibilities or fear of rejection that may result in missed opportunities or lessons. These influences are applied to the area of life or house holding and ruled by Saturn and are particularly important if Saturn rules the Ascendant or Sun sign.

If Uranus is retrograde, the native has strong inner and hidden desires to be somewhat different from others. There is a secret inner need for independence that is not often revealed. These influences are applied to area of life or house holding and ruled by Uranus and are especially important if Uranus rules the Ascendant or Sun sign.

Neptune in retrograde motion can bring the tendency towards self-deception, dishonesty, or self-destruction. This somewhat diminishes the need for escapism associated with this planet. Intuition may not be as highly developed as it would if Neptune were direct. These influences are applied to the house holding or ruled by Neptune and are especially important if Neptune rules the Ascendant or Sun sign.

When Pluto is retrograde, powerful inner strength is evident. Renewal, regeneration and recovery are available to the individual by drawing upon on inner resources. These influences are applied to the area of life or house holding or ruled by Pluto and is especially important if Pluto rules the Ascendant or Sun sign.

Interceptions

Depending on the house system used, a chart may contain intercepted signs within a house. When a house is empty and contains an intercepted sign, the secondary ruler of this house is the ruler of the intercepted sign. The planetary ruler of the empty house in question can be positioned in an intercepted sign contained within a house. When this occurs, the planetary ruler is the recipient of more than one influence and its energies are directed inwards.

Affairs of an intercepted house are generally complicated in interpreting as well as experiencing throughout life. The intercepted ruler of an empty house can provide much deeper insight of a psychological nature related to the area of life ruled by the empty house in question. The sign holding the intercepted ruler possesses the traits that can bring success to that area of life in question ruled by the empty house. The strength of an intercepted ruler is somewhat weaker, however, it still exerts influence and provides valuable information. Intercepted signs always come in pairs as the opposite sign is also intercepted.

Intercepted Planets as Empty House Rulers

An intercepted Sun indicates a feeling of emptiness within and a tendency towards introversion. This native may experience difficulties or limitations when it comes to expressing the individuality and personal potential. This is most evident in the area of life ruled by the empty house with Leo on the cusp. Traits of the Sun sign can be lacking or blocked.

An intercepted Moon can indicate emotional blockages or frustrations. Feelings of rejection can be magnified as well as experiencing a lack or confusion regarding emotional expression, understanding and compatibility. This is most evident in the area of life ruled by the empty house with Cancer on the cusp.

An intercepted Mercury can reveal a blocked intellect or limited communicative skills. The individual can often feel misunderstood and keeps most ideas and opinions within. This is most evident in the area of life ruled by the empty house with Gemini or Virgo on the cusp.

An intercepted Venus indicates frustrations, limitations and reversals within the social or romantic area. Discovering a creative outlet can remedy these setbacks. This is most evident in the area of life ruled by the empty house with Taurus or Libra on the cusp.

An intercepted Mars reveals blocked energy or thwarted drive and ambition, perhaps due to a fear of failure. High energies require a safe and sound outlet. Aggression and initiative may be lacking. This is most evident in the area of life ruled by the empty house with Aries on the cusp.

An intercepted Jupiter may hinder enthusiasm and optimism. Opportunities may be missed in life due to laziness or over-confidence. This is most evident in the area of life ruled by the empty house with Sagittarius on the cusp.

An intercepted Saturn indicates that there is an aspect or area of life that the native refuses to face, confront, or handle. Until the individual comes to terms with this inhibition, personal fulfillment will not be achieved. This is most evident in the area of life ruled by the empty house with Capricorn on the cusp.

An intercepted Uranus can result in limitations to the individuality, creativity and uniqueness of the individual. Expression of originality may be lacking. This is most evident in the area of life ruled by the empty house with Aquarius on the cusp.

An intercepted Neptune can bring a desire for escapism, privacy and seclusion. Creativity and intuition may be blocked or hindered. This is most evident in the area of life ruled by the empty house with Pisces on the cusp.

An intercepted Pluto indicates limited motives or urges. A need to grow and transform is hampered but strong. This is most evident in the area of life ruled by the empty house with Scorpio on the cusp.

Forecasting

The qualities, conditions, opportunities, obstacles and challenges in a particular house or area of life are experienced when triggered by a transit, progression, or lunation.

For example, if the ruler of the second house is positioned in the tenth and is well aspected by transit, progression or lunation, it can indicate a time of a promotion at work with a financial increase. Monetary rewards can also be realized through a parent, older individuals, or those in positions of authority. By knowing this beforehand, it would be a favorable time to expand or invest in the career and seek a promotion or raise.

If the ruler of the third house is positioned in the ninth and is adversely aspected by a transit, progression, or lunation, it can bring undesired consequences while traveling, whether short or long distance, as ruled by these houses. It could also bring negative conditions related to matters of education, publishing, law, writing, religion, communication, siblings and foreign dealings. By knowing this beforehand, it would be a favorable time to postpone travel and avoiding changes within such third and ninth house matters.

Empty First House

The Ascendant is indicative of the expression and personality projected to the world. It is the window to the soul regardless if there are planets positioned here or not. If this house is vacant, we analyze the placing of the ruler of the rising sign as it is positioned throughout the zodiac. This planet becomes the ruler of the chart and most significant in influence and individuality, health, mannerisms, appearance and the physical body of the chart owner. The sign on the first house modifies the first impression you make upon others; it is the traits of this sign and not the Sun sign that influences the appearance the most. It is how one projects the self to others. The sign and house where the chart ruler is positioned indicates how and where the individuality is best expressed. This sign modifies the personality and appearance. In other words, an empty Aries rising chart with Mars in Leo, is more than likely to exhibit physical Leonine traits.

The interpretations below are particularly important as we are discussing the ruler of the empty first house, otherwise known as the ruler and most important house of the chart. The first house is also the rising sign or Ascendant of the native. The planet ruling this sign is most influential. If two people have the same planet in the same sign, but in the chart of one that planet is also the chart ruler or ruler of the first house, then the delineation becomes much more significant in this chart than that of the other person's, whose chart is not ruled by that planet.

Empty Aries Ascendant

This individual is active, enthusiastic, courageous, extroverted and daring. The personality is somewhat self-centered, independent, competitive and impulsive. The native can be assertive, argumentative and restless. There is courage and initiative; however, difficulties in carrying a project to its end is likely. The tendency to urgently express the personality through action and energy is evident.

Mars Through the Houses

Second House: The personality is likely colored by actions and energies geared toward the acquisition of possessions, earnings, luxuries, material and financial security. Self-worth is based upon material goods. Gains can be realized through personal and aggressive efforts. This individual can be financially reckless and an impulsive spender. As the Ascendant influences the physical appearance and health, this placing can bring a Taurean appearance as well as a strong, loud voice or health problems related to the throat area.

Third House: This individual expends much energy commuting and communicating. The mind is active, versatile and fast. The tendency to switch topics midway through a sentence while abandoning an idea only to be inspired by another short-lived one is likely. An interest in debates, writing and/or teaching is likely, as well as arguments with siblings or neighbors. Opinions are expressed enthusiastically and with headstrong determination. The ability to influence others through verbal persuasion is evident. Manner of communicating can be assertive or aggressive.

Fourth House: Much energy is expended in the home and domestic realm. Arguments are likely with a close family member or parent. An active home life is likely where the native tends to run the household independently, which could produce constant domestic disputes. Fires in the home should be especially watched for.

Fifth House: This native is active in the pursuit of romantic relationships as fun and challenges in this area are eagerly sought. Healthy competition within the love life is often welcomed as impulses are often followed. Creativity is emphasized, as is the need for entertainment. Health wise, the back and heart should be free from physical exertion throughout life especially if the chart owner is fond of sports as ruled by the fifth house. Losses due to impulsive gambling are possible.

Sixth House: An active work schedule and daily interaction with a sense of routine is preferred. Arguments with co-workers are to be controlled as a result of a critical nature brought on by this house traditionally ruled by Virgo. This placing indicates a hard and tireless worker or employee. In matters of health, as ruled by this house, the head area is to be delicate and accidents should be watched for to this area.

Seventh House: This placing can indicate a troubled or active marriage or business partnership plagued by arguments. This individual may marry early or to one with an Aries or Libra Sun, Moon and/or Ascendant, or to one who has Venus and/or Mars rising or setting. The individual can be somewhat self-centered when it comes to marriage or partnerships due to a strong need for challenge and independence within these relationships.

Eighth House: An active sex drive is likely a strong part of this personality as emotions are highly passionate and must be expressed in a physical manner. Dealings with other's finances, such as loans, taxes and inheritances are likely frequent. This placing benefits such occupations as banking, investing, the stock market and financial advising. Financial changes due to marriage or partnerships are likely to be experienced.

Ninth House: Active involvement with institutions of learning, worship, teaching, publishing or travel is likely. An explorative nature with a need to travel and expand mental horizons is likely. The mentality can be philosophically and spiritually inclined, as well as alert and clear. Thoughts are impulsive and independent from others. Arguments or difficulties can arise while abroad.

Tenth House: This brings a career-oriented native who may choose the military, carpentry, athletics, firefighting, sports or operating machinery. Arguments with a parent, superiors or those in authority are likely. It is important for this native to experience freedom and challenges within the career. An aggressive outlook is evident, particularly when it comes to achieving professional goals and a solid reputation. This individual enjoys being in command at the workplace; orders may be hard to follow.

Eleventh House: Much energy is expended into making hopes and dreams come true. There can be much activity involving groups, clubs, organizations and friendships. Friends can be aggressive, forceful or opinionated and therefore, arguments often result. This is the mark of a social leader and active humanitarian.

Twelfth House: The need for action, motivation, activity and energy may be lacking. This individual can be moody, reclusive, introverted and self-sacrificing. There is often involvement with secretive or behind the scenes activity. This placing hinders assertiveness or aggressiveness and it could bring secret enemies or the native's self-undoing. Esoteric astrologers believe that Mars (if the sole planet in the twelfth house) in this position is indicative of the previous incarnation as being a male.

Empty Taurus Ascendant

This individual is persistent, reliable, self-indulgent, loyal and dependable. The personality is also rational but can be somewhat stubborn or self-centered. Nature is calm and relaxed. The native does not jump to conclusions and is most careful and patient in all matters. A love of the finer things in life, such as jewelry, art, rich foods and fashion is likely. Attachment to financial or material possessions can be strong.

Venus Through the Houses

Second House: This individual enjoys the finer things in life, which can bring material security or financial self-worth. Purchases of an aesthetic value are often made. Financial acquisitions are well thought out and planned and earning potential is well developed. There is an attraction to money that is not spent foolishly. There is willingness to work hard and steadily to acquire financial security.

Third House: This individual enjoys communicating to the fullest, whether verbally or in writing. Mental stimulation with others is eagerly sought. A love of literature and poetry is evident as this placing produces imaginative writers and speakers. Close ties with siblings and same generation relatives are likely. Feelings are often verbally expressed and words tend to be carefully chosen.

Fourth House: A strong affection for the home and family life is evident as there is a close bond with family members and the parent ruled by this house. (Chapter IV explains how to determine which house rules which parent.) The home is likely decorated with lovely furniture and accessories. In later years, an inheritance is likely received in the form of property or land.

Fifth House: This placing often brings a love of children, fun, social life, entertainment, gambling and romantic pursuits. Creative and artistic ability is likely if this talent is pursued and developed. Many romantic opportunities are available as this placing cannot help but attract romantic potentials.

Sixth House: This placing often brings interest in health and dietary matters. The personality is best expressed through the work. There can be popularity among co-workers and many friends and lovers are met or formed through the work place. There is little difficulty finding work. This placing often indicates a fondness for pets.

Seventh House: Emotional fulfillment is experienced through personal relationships. This native tends to see themselves through the eyes of others due to the polarity of the first and seventh houses. When involved in an important relationship is when this individual feels complete. Partnerships are based on affection and admiration whether romantic or business. The finances are often affected due to the marriage or partnership. Marriage tends to come early in life due to the native's popularity. Compatibility is found with one who has the Sun, Moon and/or Ascendant in Taurus or Scorpio as well as with Venus and/or Pluto rising or setting.

Eighth House: Physical charm and charisma attracts many romantic partners. Secrets or mystery often surround the romantic life. There is an interest in research, the mysteries of life and the acquisition of finances through others. Finances can be affected through matters related to the deceased, such as inheritances, legacies, insurance and wills.

Ninth House: There is interest in philosophy, higher learning, spirituality, religion, foreign cultures or languages, as well as long distance travel. A marriage or partnership can result with a foreigner or perhaps encountered while abroad. The marriage itself may take place far away from home. Success and romance can be realized through publishing ventures, institutions of higher learning and religious studies.

Tenth House: Financial gain is likely through personal career efforts. Professional goals are most important. Honors and success can be realized through women and/or Venus-ruled professions such as art, beauty, jewelry, cosmetics, fashion, finances, architecture, dance, design, entertainment and music. This can be a very good placing for career successes. This individual can charm their way up the professional ladder. Romantic relations with older individuals are likely as well as with a boss, superior, or through professional contacts or connections.

Eleventh House: Lasting, stable and dependable friendships are likely formed. Friends are many, mostly female and often cultured and refined. Emotional or romantic relationships are often formed with friends. A friend can be become a lover or introduce the potential lover to the native. Friendships can also be financially rewarding.

Twelfth House: Secret romantic relationships of a sacrificial or deeply emotional nature are often attracted. There is fondness for seclusion, privacy and secrecy. This is the mark of the eccentric artist who requires time alone, behind the scenes while escaping through a highly creative outlet. This placing protects the native from enemies. If Venus is the only planet in this house, the native was likely a female in the past incarnation.

Empty Gemini Ascendant

A Gemini rising personality is talkative, flexible and restless with a sparkling personality. This is a very changeable and extroverted individual who often shows two sides. A busy and varied lifestyle is sought as boredom can easily set it. The manner of expression is versatile, inquisitive and expressive. Seldom, is the native at a loss for words. Contacts, communication and interaction with others are often sought. Interests are many and often, more than one are handled at the same time.

Mercury Through the Houses

Second House: The native may often discuss finances with others. The personality is projected through the acquisition of finances and material security. The earning potential can strengthen through such professions as writing, teaching, salesmanship, lecturing, as well as those within the communication or travel industry. Mercury, being a dual sign, may bring to this individual more than one source of income.

Third House: There is much communicative ability and talent for writing. There is a need for study as the mind is inquisitive, sharp, quick and easily able to grasp details and knowledge. Exchanging ideas or simply communicating with siblings and close relatives is important. Mercury, as planet of travel, in the third house of short distance travel, indicates much coming and going.

Fourth House: This placing often brings much communication within the family and domestic circle. Problems in this area can be talked out, however, many arguments are also likely. Unstable home conditions or early home life is indicated due to the changeable nature of this planet. Many changes of residence are also indicated. Literary activities such as writing, reading, or teaching are often enjoyed from the home and can bring benefits. This can be a good placing for selling land, property, real estate, domestic and food products.

Fifth House: This individual is most self-expressive and verbally creative. Relationships are most important and tend to predominate thoughts. Verbal interaction is vital in romantic relationships. As this placing is conducive to teaching or conversing with children, the native can excel as a grade school teacher. Potential lovers must first capture the mind for the relationship to have potential. Lovers are many and often younger in age. There is a strong need for variety and change as boredom and restlessness can quickly set in this area.

Sixth House: A tendency for excessive talking at the work place is likely with this placing. Native enjoys exchanging thoughts and ideas with others, particularly with co-workers and on a daily basis. Work involving writing can be successful as well as traveling and teaching. The mind should avoid worry, stress and overwork as an active mentality can affect the nervous system, as this house rules health matters.

Seventh House: More than one marriage is indicated when a dual sign such as Gemini rises or sets. Mental compatibility and communication is crucial to successful major relationships, however instability is also likely in this area. There is often an attraction or important relationships, such as marriage or partnership, formed with those of an intellectual or literary nature. The spouse or partner is most likely younger in years.

Eighth House: This placing often reveals interest in studying occult or hidden subjects. The native tends to be verbally expressive about matters of sex or death. The mentality is sharp, alert and penetrating. Manner of communicating can be somewhat secretive or mysterious. This native is curious and enjoys a good mystery. This placing benefits research and investigation.

Ninth House: This is an excellent placing for higher learning, publishing, travel, writing, journalism, lecturing and teaching. Different cultures and languages are easily absorbed, as the intellect is deep, probing, curious and hungry for knowledge. Philosophical conversations are often enjoyed as well as interests of an intellectual or cultural nature.

Tenth House: Often, this indicates one lives for a career. A Mercurial profession such as editing, administrative work, travel industry, lecturing, reporting, bookkeeping, writing, teaching or any work requiring verbal and/or mental skills are best suited. Professional success is likely as well as an elevated status in life.

Eleventh House: Friendships are most important to this native as the personality is socially minded. There is likely much activity and participation with groups, clubs, or organizations. Friends are often younger and tend to be of the intellectual or literary type. Although many friendships are likely formed, they seem to be fickle or lacking in permanence or endurance.

Twelfth House: Communicative skills, thoughts and ideas are best expressed behind the scenes or in privacy. Intuition and compassion is highly developed. Problems are carefully thought out and kept private. The subconscious mind is active, however, the energy is directed inwards. This placing can increase nervous strain or tension. There can be a sense or fear of being imprisoned by thoughts and ideas that can also bring the native's undoing. This is an excellent placing for research or detective work.

Empty Cancer Ascendant

This native is receptive, caring, family-oriented and intuitive. Emotionally, the personality is sympathetic, intense and nurturing. There are strong emotional ties with either the mother, a relative, or within the domestic life. Family traditions are held in great respect and importance. Imagination is strong and an introverted personality is likely. Deep feelings tend to be kept hidden within and criticism is not handled well.

The Moon Through the Houses

Second House: Emotional fulfillment and security is acquired through possessions and material gains. Due to the Moon's changeable nature, fluctuating finances are to be expected as earning can go just as easily as they come to this individual. Earning potential is best expressed through Lunar-ruled professions such as catering, hotel/restaurant industry, nursing, domestic services, or dealing with the public.

Third House: A close emotional bond with a sibling or a same-generation relative is likely. A strong imagination, sharp memory and a quick mind are to be expected as well as an intellect strongly influenced by emotions, intuition and hunches. Many journeys are expected. Learning ability is well developed as knowledge is easily retained. Manner of communicating can be sympathetic and caring.

Fourth House: The Moon is well placed here as it is in its natural home. Family ties are pronounced and the tendency to be protective of the family is indicated. A close bond with a parent, more likely the mother as ruled by the Moon, is evident. Happiness is found within a pleasant and comfortable home and surroundings where peaceful time alone can also be enjoyed. The inconstant Moon can bring frequent changes of residence. A home by the water is likely during early or later years. Emotions are strong but can often be repressed.

Fifth House: This individual is fun loving and will likely experience many romantic alliances throughout life. The native can be over-protective and highly possessive of lovers. A torch may still burn for past romances. Relationships may lack consistency with the Moon in this house. A close bond with children is evident however, the tendency to be critical or possessive of them should be avoided.

Sixth House: This individual can adapt well as an employee and easily relate to co-workers. The tendency to be involved in a service to the public is evident. The ever-changing Moon in this placing can bring many changes of work throughout life. Health can also fluctuate and the stomach area can be delicate.

Seventh House: This placing indicates one who sees themselves through the eyes of others, particularly in a spouse or partner. Emotions can be strongly influenced or triggered by others. There can be much popularity and dealings with the public. Security needs are often met through personal relationships as deep emotional fulfillment is derived from being in a long-term relationship. The partner must provide a powerful emotional bond, security and protection. This individual can be protective or possessive with the spouse or partner. Compatibility is found with one who has Sun, Moon and/or Ascendant in Cancer or Capricorn as well as the Moon and/or Saturn rising or setting.

Eighth House: This individual is deep feeling, secretive, emotional and highly sexual. An inheritance from the mother, the maternal side of the family, or females in general is likely. Finances can also be affected through a marriage or business partnership. Emotional changes and personal transformations are often experienced. A hurt or act of kindness is never forgotten. It is next to impossible to keep a secret from this native.

Ninth House: This individual can excel at teaching others and pursuing a higher education. There is often an attraction to and interest in travel, law, philosophy, religion, foreign languages or cultures. Emotional fulfillment can be attained through expanding the mind into new horizons of much higher levels.

Tenth House: Status and career ambitions are of utmost importance to this native. Recognition within the community or profession is likely. This individual can excel in such careers as the restaurant and food industry, nursing, domestic services and real estate. A woman may be of considerable importance regarding the career or status. A close bond with the mother is evident. The fluctuating Moon can bring frequent changes within the profession throughout life.

Eleventh House: Friends are most important to this native as is participation with groups, clubs, or organizations. Close friends, mostly females, are often considered as family and the mother or family members can also become good friends. There is often a life-long relationship with a childhood friend. Inconsistent, fluctuating, or changeable friends are likely.

Twelfth House: Much time is enjoyed in seclusion perhaps accompanied by private thoughts and the entertainment of subconscious messages. This individual enjoys a good mystery. Interest in occult subjects is likely. Compassion is highly developed as well as the tendency toward secrecy and behind-the-scenes activity. Powerful feelings may be repressed or hidden from others due to a highly sensitive nature that is easily hurt. This placing tends to be indicative of a most recent life lived as a woman.

Empty Leo Ascendant

This placing indicates one who is cheerful, outgoing, generous, proud and romantic. The personality is affectionate and dignified as well as strong and prone to dominate others. This is an excellent placing for leading or acting as a powerful need for approval and attention is evident. This position reveals little or no modesty. This individual is creative and organized with a flair for drama and enjoys being the center of attention. Sense of humor is well developed. This individual understands children. There is a tendency to dramatize events and emotions. There is great creative potential with a strong need for approval, appreciation and encouragement.

The Sun Through the Houses

Second House: Those in positions of influence and authority can further the native's financial and material goals. This individual enjoys spending money on fine and luxurious objects that can be proudly displayed. The tendency is toward being generous with finances. Self-worth and emotional security is achieved through the acquisition of possessions and material wealth.

Third House: Communication is very important to this individual. A busy life is likely, as the native is sociable, talkative and restless. Close ties and much communication with siblings or same-generation relatives are evident. The mind is curious, studious and intellectual. Success can be achieved through writing, travel, communications, teaching and lecturing. Optimism and a sense of humor are also evident.

Fourth House: The native must rule or dominate within the domestic environment. A relative or a parent plays an important role in the life of this individual. A sense of family pride tends to come with this placing. This individual can be highly emotional and outspoken when it comes to family issues. There is a tendency to cling to the past.

Fifth House: The native's outgoing nature is emphasized with this placing. Fun, socializing and romance predominates most of this native's thoughts, plans and actions. Playful and fun loving, this (Leo rising with the Sun in the fifth house) is the classic "Child of the Zodiac." Much fondness and affection for children and offspring is evident.

Sixth House: Individuality and self-expression is best channeled through the job or workplace. The native is at best when busy at work or performing a service for others. Reassurance of a job well done and recognition fuels this individual's energy. The health can be delicate and may require extra attention. Routine is handled well and attention to detail is most precise, being a valuable asset at the workplace.

Seventh House: This individual feels complete when involved in a meaningful relationship. Complete satisfaction is sought through companionship and interaction with others; many close relationships are likely. However with Aquarius here, the union must provide sufficient freedom and unpredictability as routine and monotony can destroy relationships. The natives tend to see themselves through the eyes of others, particularly when the Sun mirrors the chart's Ascendant. It would be best to not allow others to interfere with or direct the personal life. Compatibility is achieved with one who has Leo or Aquarius Sun, Moon and/or Ascendant as well as having the Sun and/or Uranus rising or setting.

Eighth House: Individuality is best expressed through physically romantic relationships where all is given and nothing is held back. The native can be intensely secretive and sexual. A sense of personal transformation or re-birth can be achieved through these physical relationships. The career may involve the handling of other's finances, as well as professions related to secrecy, death, sex, research, or investigation. An inheritance is likely and financial gains or losses through a marriage or partnership are evident.

Ninth House: The individuality is best expressed through such matters as higher learning, foreign cultures, law, religion, publishing and distant travel. Goals often involve the expansion of the intellect as well as spiritual, philosophic, or cultural horizons. The personality is optimistic and a great sense of humor is likely.

Tenth House: This placing increases the chances of a successful career with a prominent position. By exerting little effort, this native can succeed and reach an honorable position of authority or status. There is a tremendous drive for success and recognition. This individual is able to rise above the rest through an outgoing personality and creative talent that can result in a self-made individual.

Eleventh House: This individual is very popular and well liked among groups, organizations and particularly with friendships that are many. Friends are often outgoing, fun loving and adventurous. Humanitarian causes may be of interest. The native can excel as a group leader. Many hopes and wishes can come true and benefits or losses through friends and group participation can also be expected.

Twelfth House: Leo rising individuals enjoy attention and being in the spotlight. However with the Sun in the twelfth house, the personality is much more private, secretive, reclusive and introverted. Self doubt or lack of self-confidence can hinder progress. Interest in mysticism is likely. The individuality can be well expressed through charitable, healing, or hospital work. Self-sacrifice, self-delusion and unhealthy escapism should strongly be avoided. This placing is often indicative of living a most recent life as man.

Empty Virgo Ascendant

This individual can be highly discriminating, detail-oriented and critical. There is much concern with neatness, hygiene and organization. The world must always be in some type of perfect order with everything in its logical place. The mind is incisive but can also tend toward fault-finding and excessive worry. Common sense, keen observation and deep analysis are applied when making important choices and decisions.

Mercury Through the Houses

Second House: This individual is concerned with possessions, finances and the acquisition of material goods. Deep analysis and keen observation can be applied toward reaching financial goals. Money-making ideas can be formed and expressed to others.

Third House: This individual enjoys conversations and communication with siblings and same-generation relatives. However, the tendency toward being over critical or over analytical with these people should be avoided. Acute mental faculties are likely as well as a great need to communicate. It is as if the mind never shuts down with this placing. The native can be prone to worry, gossip and always seems be on the go. This is a good position for a writer or teacher.

Fourth House: Home, family, roots and domestic ties are of prime importance. Frequent changes of residence are likely. This is a good placing for conducting business within the home or involvement in careers dealing with domestic products, hotel and food industry, real estate, land or property dealings. It is important to have clear and open communication within the family.

Fifth House: When it comes to selecting romantic partners, this personality is most discriminative and choosy. Decisions and choices involving matters of the heart are made from the intellect as opposed to from the emotions. This placing tends to bring younger romantic partners. Intellectual rapport is essential when it comes to romantic compatibility. Permanence and stability, due to the changeable nature of Mercury, can be somewhat lacking as boredom can easily set in this area. The tendency to be over critical and fault-finding with children and lovers is to be avoided.

Sixth House: This individual is hard working and can be a most efficient employee. An interest in health, diet and hygiene is evident. The mentality can be nervous, analytical and prone to worry. A job involving writing, teaching or communication can bring success and personal satisfaction. Gossip and excessive talking within the workplace can bring reversals with co-workers.

Seventh House: Much verbal interaction and intellectual rapport is required from the spouse or partner, as communication is vital to all close relationships. Often this partner if younger in age or intellectual or literary. The tendency to be swayed by others should be avoided. Long-term romantic compatibility is best found with another who has Virgo or Pisces Sun, Moon and/or Ascendant as well as Mercury and/or Neptune rising or setting.

Eighth House: This native is likely involved with the finances of others. Conversations or debates often involve such topics as sex, death and the mysteries of life. The mind is suited to furthering education regarding such interests. This is a good placing for a financial speaker, spokesperson, advisor, or researcher.

Ninth House: This is the mark of the philosopher, the teacher and the eternal student, forever questioning life and seeking higher knowledge. Many long trips abroad are likely. The native may speak several languages due to the remarkable ability to master foreign languages and their cultures. The mentality tends to be explorative, critical, alert, literary and optimistic.

Tenth House: The personality is best expressed through career and professional matters. It is a good placing for an employer, boss, or superior. Ambitions are strong as is the need for a respected status. The dual nature of Mercury can bring two careers when placed in this house. Professional success can be realized in the fields of accounting, nutrition, health, dentistry, nursing and pharmaceuticals.

Eleventh House: Feelings and communication are constantly shared and expressed among friendships and within group associations. Friends are often younger individuals and carefully scrutinized as those of an intellectual or literary nature are often selected. Friends may come and go due to the changeable and fickle nature of Mercury here.

Twelfth House: Here is a Virgo rising individual that can keep a secret and is less prone to gossip. Thoughts, ideas and opinions are often kept private and periods of seclusion are required in order to replenish this highly active subconscious mind. Much time is spent in deep thought and intuition can be a valuable tool. However, there is often difficulty in expressing or communicating emotions. The tendency toward critical self-analysis and worrying over inconsequential matters and details should be avoided as it could bring the native's self-undoing.

Empty Libra Ascendant

This individual is diplomatic, fair, impartial and refined. This placing tends to bring an attractive appearance, charm and grace. Peace and harmony is essential for well-being and cursing, rude, or vulgar behavior or language is strongly disliked. Artistic talent or interest is likely. Social interaction, approval and acceptance from others are important and because of this, indecision can be the result. Both sides of issues are able to be clearly seen or distinguished however, frequently weighing the pros and cons of every decision can hinder progress. The need for companionship is emphasized as the native can feel lost when in alone or in solitude.

Venus Through the Houses

Second House: This individual is fond of elegant and refined possessions and luxuries. The financial status is of considerable importance and the native may be motivated by financial goals. There is the tendency to become somewhat materialistic, as it is important for the native to exude an impression of wealth and sophisticated taste. There is little hesitation in spending on the finer things in life that enhance the appearance and close environment.

Third House: Words are carefully chosen and expressed most eloquently. The tendency to avoid arguments is evident as pleasant and peaceful conversations are sought. Romance can be encountered while on short distance travels, or through siblings, same generation relatives, or neighbors. This individual enjoys talking about romance. Venus in this house indicates the possibility of success as a romance writer, columnist, or counselor.

Fourth House: The home must be elegant and filled with luxurious items. Get-togethers at the home are often enjoyed. Peace and harmony within the domestic circle is essential for this native's well being as family discord is strongly disliked. There is strong affection for the parent ruled by this house. Gains through property, land, or a family inheritance can take place in later years.

Fifth House: Romantic partners are often selected for their good looks and charm. Many romantic potentials are attracted due to the native's fun and outgoing personality. There is fondness for children and a strong need for fun, entertainment and an active social life. A creative hobby can further financial goals.

Sixth House: The individual uses charm and charisma when seeking a job. Romances with co-workers or with individuals encountered through the job are likely. This personality strives for harmonious and pleasant relations and environment while at work; however, the tendency to be manipulated or easily influenced by co-workers should be watched for. The liver and kidney area may require attention as this is the house of health. There is much fondness for pets.

Seventh House: This personality feels complete only when involved in a serious and harmonious relationship. Love and a happy marriage or partnership is of paramount importance to this native. Emotional balance and happiness largely depends upon others, specifically the spouse or partner. There is danger of losing the self-identity through others or within these relationships. As Aries falls on this cusp, the spouse is more independent and self-oriented from which this native can learn and benefit. Long-term compatibility can be found with another who has Aries or Libra Sun, Moon and/or Ascendant as well as Venus and/or Mars rising or setting.

Eighth House: Physical passions are strong and highly emotional. Romantically, this native best expresses affections in a physical manner. Financial gains or losses through a partner or spouse are likely as well as through inheritances and dealings with other's finances. There can be a love of mystery, a strong interest in sex and curiosity about death and the afterlife.

Ninth House: This native is attracted to foreigners or tends to encounter romance while on long distance travel. Romance can also be found through institutions of higher learning. The spouse or partner is likely from another country. There is much fondness for travel, expanding the mind, as well as interests in such topics as philosophy, foreign cultures, law, religion and spirituality.

Tenth House: This native may be married to the career or falls in love with a superior, boss or older, more established individual. Marrying into money is not ruled out. Careers that can bring success include art, cosmetics, jewelry, designing and law. Through charm, diplomacy, good looks, artistic talents and popularity with the public, can this individual rise in status. Women can be instrumental in reaching career goals. There is a strong bond with the parent ruled by this house.

Eleventh House: There is much fondness for friendships, particularly those female and group endeavors. Those chosen are cultural with refined tastes and personalities. This individual enjoys matchmaking friends with each other and the native can be introduced by a friend to a future spouse or partner. Romantic partners can easily become friends and a friend may become a spouse or partner. Social or financial goals can be furthered or disrupted by friendships.

Twelfth House: This Libra rising individual is not as social as others with this placing. There is a tendency to be private, reclusive and highly introspective. Secret relationships are often attracted or romantic partners themselves tend to be of an illusive nature. This placing tends to indicate a love of a good mystery and a most recent life lived as a woman. This is the house of hidden enemies and there can be attraction, fondness, or fascination with those considered as such. Venus also brings protection from enemies when in the twelfth house as result of past life actions.

Empty Scorpio Ascendant

This individual is emotionally intense, private and resourceful. When needed, there is an ability to draw upon hidden strengths and resources. Will and perseverance is admirable and charisma can be strong. Desires are intense, however if betrayed, the sting of a Scorpio will never be forgotten. Emotional manipulation and control should be avoided. There is an interest or attraction to mysteries and secrets.

Pluto Through the Houses

Second House: This individual exerts much personal energy and power into the acquisition of financial or material security. It is important to be in total control over the finances. The native is not afraid to take risks in the financial area. A personal transformation can take place through the gains or losses of wealth and material goods.

Third House: This native can be quite verbally persuasive and commanding when communicating with others. Personal inner growth and change may result through the interchange of ideas and thoughts, particularly with siblings or through writing. The mind is deep, penetrating and probing, constantly seeking to solve problems and mysteries. This personality may be prone to being suspicious of others. Secrets are well kept and may involve a sibling or same generation relative.

Fourth House: This individual needs to dominate or be in control within the domestic environment. There can be a secret or mystery surrounding the childhood, a parent, or close relative. The parent represented by this house is likely to exert a powerful and controlling effect or hold upon this individual. Family betrayals are not forgotten.

Fifth House: This individual possesses tremendous energy and resourcefulness, particularly when dealing with children, romantic interests, or when expressing a creative talent or interest. Much physical passion coupled with an active romantic life is indicated. Power struggles can also arise within romantic relationships or when relating to children.

Sixth House: This individual requires a certain amount of control at the workplace. Power struggles and resentments in this area can rise due to suspicious or jealous tendencies. Secret relationships with co-workers are likely. There can also be an element of secrecy involving the job. The native is a tireless worker who can be manipulative when achieving employment goals.

Seventh House: It has been said that this placing is indicative of many previous incarnations, all which have been transformed by long-term relationships. Each separation or ending within a marriage or partnership can be traumatic, resulting in greater inner personal transformation. The native is never the same after each break-up as the character strengthens each time. This individual is strong willed and hard to control by others. Developing the technique of compromise will greatly relieve troubles within the marriage or partnership. This individual often attracts powerful personalities. Deep romantic commitment is achieved through another who has Taurus or Scorpio Sun, Moon and/or Ascendant, or with Venus and/or Pluto rising or setting.

Eighth House: This individual is capable of great physical passion. Emotions are deeply felt and as a result, the native often experiences a rebirth or personal transformation. There is a tendency to be suspicious when it comes to finances and matters such as death, sex, the afterlife and other's finances. Matters requiring research and investigation are handled with skill. There is an element of secrecy or mystery surrounding the personality.

Ninth House: Higher learning, the quest for deeper knowledge and emotional intensity brings personal growth and inner transformation. Intellectual boundaries are fearlessly explored and expanded. This placing heightens intuition. There is often an interest in mysteries, other cultures and occult philosophies or ideas.

Tenth House: A powerful personality with leadership or domineering tendencies is likely. Ambitions hold neither boundaries nor fears to this native. The reputation and career is likely to experience several transformations or major changes, where rebuilding from scratch is necessary. This placing benefits such professions as private investigation, gynecology, surgery, research, physics, tax consulting, psychiatry, psychology, plumbing, police work and within the military field.

Eleventh House: When it comes to friendships and group associations, this native must be in complete control. This individual can be a successful social reformer or powerful group leader where great will, perseverance and magnetic charm are required. The native can be suspicious or jealous of friends or of those involved in the same groups or organizations. Secret friendships are likely formed.

Twelfth House: This individual is intensely secretive and introspective. Deep hidden feelings are kept within. Enormous hidden resources can be tapped into for personal growth and soul advancement. A strong subconscious mind and great emotional intensity describes the personality. There is much involvement either with places of confinement or behind the scenes activities. This placing would greatly benefit a psychologist or psychiatrist who is able to penetrate the secrets of the hidden intellect. As this is the house of karma, conditions from a past life likely have a powerful effect upon the present subconscious.

Empty Sagittarius Ascendant

This personality is optimistic, honest, fun loving, outgoing and has a good sense of humor and adventure. The native is generous, friendly, philosophic, sincere and has high aspirations. A philosophical or spiritual attitude as well as an open mind is likely. Freedom and independence is highly desired. There is fondness for the outdoors, animals and sports. The tendency towards being blunt in speech can offend or hurt others.

Jupiter Through the Houses

Second House: This placing brings numerous financial opportunities. If this house is ruled by Capricorn, the ability to acquire and accumulate financial and material rewards is likely through hard work, patience and personal efforts. The tendency toward being too generous or too stingy with finances should be avoided.

Third House: Success can come through matters involving teaching, law, writing, short distance travel, siblings and communication in general. This individual is optimistic, honest and straightforward, however, an over-confident mind or attitude can bring reversals. The ability to learn foreign languages is present as the intellect is most eager to learn. Many siblings are likely with whom good relations are maintained.

Fourth House: A large and fun-loving family is likely as well as a happy childhood and a rewarding end of life. This individual can find successful opportunities in matters such as real estate, domestic products or services, or the hotel and restaurant industry. Opportunities and benefits, such as an inheritance, may also come from the parent represented by this house. A home in a foreign land during later years is likely.

Fifth House: The native may experience many financially rewarding opportunities. However, being overly generous or taking risks with money can bring reversals. Rewards and happiness can also come through creative endeavors and children, whom are often many. The social life is expansive and many romantic partners are likely. Sense of humor is evident as well as the need for fun and adventure. This individual can be fond of animals, gambling, risky sports, games and hobbies.

Sixth House: Luck and opportunities can arise through the workplace, co-workers, or by being of service to others. This individual is able to raise the moral and bring humor when at work. Good health is likely, however there can be setbacks to the liver area as ruled by Jupiter. This native has no problem exploring the many opportunities for work that are often encountered.

Seventh House: This placing can bring luck, happiness and several opportunities within the marriage or partnership area, as more than one union is likely. Being overly generous or too confident can bring reversals within these relationships. Compatibility is achieved with another who has Gemini or Sagittarius Sun, Moon, or Ascendant. Or to one who has Mercury or Jupiter rising or setting in the chart.

Eighth House: This individual has a healthy and optimistic attitude toward sex, death and life's mysteries. Financial rewards and opportunities are likely gained or lost through a marriage or partnership. Many opportunities involving the finances of others such as dealings with inheritances, legacies, wills, loans, or taxes are evident.

Ninth House: This native can strongly benefit from higher learning, journalism, teaching, publishing and foreign interests. The intellect is optimistic, expansive and probing. There is a flair for languages and a good sense of humor. This individual tends to be philosophical, spiritual, religious and morally conscious. Rewarding experiences can be realized through long distance travels. This is a good placing for Jupiter, as it is its natural home.

Tenth House: This is an excellent placing for Jupiter in terms of career, goals, ambitions and status, as help from influential people is often attracted. Many rewarding opportunities are likely to come from such professions as sports, advertising, travel, foreign relations, publishing, sales, law, religion and teaching. This placing often brings increased popularity as positions of authority are well handled. As an employer, this native can be honest, optimistic and forgiving.

Eleventh House: This can be an excellent position for Jupiter; it can bring luck to the native's hopes and wishes. Benefits or worthwhile opportunities can come from friendships or group associations. This individual is popular among friends due to a generous and humorous nature. Many friends are likely formed with adventurous or outgoing people.

Twelfth House: Due to good karma, this individual is protected from danger and hidden or secret enemies. Spiritual, hospital and charitable work can bring benefits. Many secrets or mysterious involvements are attracted. Frequent opportunities for participating in secretive or behind the scenes activities are also indicated.

Empty Capricorn Ascendant

This individual is cautious, reserved, ambitious, hardworking, patient and persevering. The personality is dependable, honest and introverted. Emotions are kept well under control resulting in a serious outlook on life. Stability and sense of responsibility is well developed. Every activity or task must have a practical or useful purpose. The lessons in life are indicated by analyzing the position of Saturn, the planet of karma, in the horoscope.

Saturn Through the Houses

Second House: This personality is persevering and hardworking when it comes to making money. Financial ambition is combined with an element of shrewdness as stability in this area is important. Gains can be slow but worthwhile. This placing does not produce a reckless spender, as the tendency toward thrift is likely. Secure financial investments can bring rewards. Life lessons involve material and financial issues as well as sense of worth.

Third House: This placing brings well-developed mental concentration and learning ability. Communication is cautious, serious and rational. A tendency for pessimism should be avoided. Emotional relationships with siblings or same generation relatives may be stressed or lack warmth and be somewhat distant. Life's lessons involve these relationships or communication in general.

Fourth House: There may have been a lack of affection during childhood as a result of a strict or unemotional parent. Many responsibilities or restrictions may also have been endured; however, the later years bring stability and security. The possibility of becoming a recluse is not ruled out. Life lessons revolve around parents, family and the domestic life.

Fifth House: This placing often indicates few offspring; however a strong karmic bond with the first child is felt. Raising children can bring extra restrictions and increased responsibilities. The tendency toward being too strict or overly cautious with children should be avoided. When dating, older partners tend to be attracted. This individual would greatly benefit by experiencing fun and letting go every once in a while, as risks are seldom taken. Life lessons involve children and romantic relationships.

Sixth House: This individual is a most efficient worker with a sound sense of duty and service. A need for respect from co-workers and subordinates is pronounced. The native seldom socializes with co-workers Working conditions and environment can be regarded as restrictive or laden with too many responsibilities. Cold or setbacks to the skin or bones in later years is likely. Overwork can also tax the health. Lessons in life involve the work and health area.

Seventh House: Marriage can be late, delayed, or regarded as restrictive due to many responsibilities that it could bring. There is an element of caution within marriage. The spouse or partner will likely be of an age difference or a reserved type of nature with Cancer or Capricorn Sun, Moon and/or Ascendant and Moon and/or Saturn rising or setting. These relationships are seldom rushed into and are not taken lightly as security is vital in this area. It has been written that this placing brings a karmic marriage or relationship with issues presently needed to be worked out as life lessons involve marriage and long-term relationships.

Eighth House: When it comes to handling other people's finances or gains; stability and rewards, or restrictions and delays, can be expected. A serious, skeptical and rational outlook on life, sex, death and matters of the occult is likely cultivated. This placing is conducive to a long life provided other aspects do not counteract this influence. Romantically, the native may be somewhat inhibited or a late bloomer. Life lessons involve the mysteries of life or the handling of other's finances.

Ninth House: Status and honors are likely achieved through higher education, philosophy, travel, law, foreign cultures, or spirituality. The intellect is deep and serious, wasting no time on superficialities or minute trivia. Spiritual poverty can also manifest with this placing. When traveling to a foreign land for the first time, the native often feels a sense of déjà vu. Life lessons involve the pursuit of higher knowledge through deep studious work, spirituality, travel, or expanding mental horizons.

Tenth House: This placing brings enough sense of responsibility to be able to assume a position of high status, authority and respect. Through ambition, patience and perseverance, will this native rise. This is often the mark of the self-made individual; however it also indicates a "rise and fall." Professional success can be realized through banking, real estate, land, dentistry, architecture and carpentry. Life lessons involve the career, status and reputation.

Eleventh House: Friendships tend to be few or lasting and of a karmic nature. Losses, delays, restrictions, or extra responsibilities can also be experienced as a result of these alliances. Regardless, those selected as friends, are serious and perhaps more mature, older, or established. Hopes and dreams can be realized through patience, determination and perseverance. Life lessons involve friendships, group involvements, hopes and dreams.

Twelfth House: This placing indicates a heavily burdened or lonely previous life that has left subconscious scars on the present. Much karmic guilt and work is therefore required to experience in order to progress. Repressed emotions can result as well as a lack of self-confidence. Restrictions can be self imposed and secret fears or sorrows can prevent growth. It is only by facing these fears and sorrows that karmic rewards can be experienced. This individual prefers working in seclusion, avoiding the harsh realities of the world. Becoming a recluse in later years is not ruled out. Life lessons are deeply rooted in karma, the subconscious and fears.

Empty Aquarius Ascendant

This individual is unconventional, motivated by inspiration, friendly, original and independent. The personality is unpredictable, honest and detached. There is a strong need to project the uniqueness of the personality. Often regarded as eccentric, the native enjoys being different from others. Others are easily attracted as the nature is magnetic, people-oriented and lively.

Uranus Through the Houses

Second House: There is something out of the ordinary about how finances and material goods are acquired or gained. Money can easily come and go, as stability is not a Uranian trait. Sudden financial windfalls or losses are likely. An unconventional attitude is taken in regards to self-worth and financial gains.

Third House: This individual possesses an individual or unique manner of learning or communicating. The intellect is bright, quick and inventive. Unconventional thoughts, great intuition and imagination are likely, however a scattered mind can bring misunderstandings or estrangement, particularly with siblings. There is something unusual about the relationships with siblings or same age relatives. Unusual experiences or encounters can be experienced through short distance travels. Accidents can also arise during trips.

Fourth House: A disruptive, unusual, or unconventional family life is likely, filled with sudden changes of residence and disruptions. Domestic ties can be somewhat distant as the nature is to be independent from the family at an early age. Changes or losses through property or real estate dealings are evident. Electrical accidents in the home should always be prevented.

Fifth House: This placing shows an abundance of creativity

coupled with a strong need for fun, excitement and romance. The romantic life is somewhat unusual or eccentric as sudden infatuations are likely, yet not enduring. Romantic affairs can begin suddenly and terminate in the same manner, as much experimentation is desired within this area. Sudden financial windfalls or losses are likely through speculation. A hobby can best bring out the native's creativity and originality.

Sixth House: Fluctuating or unusual work is often attracted. Jobs can begin as suddenly as they end, as there is a strong need to project the individuality and independence resulting in sudden job changes. This native can bring new and original ideas that can improve work methods or conditions. Unusual ties are likely formed with co-workers.

Seventh House: Much freedom and independence is required in marriage and partnerships. The spouse or partner is far from dull and the relationship must be exciting, unusual, unpredictable or even unconventional in some manner. Compatibility is found with one who has Leo or Aquarius Sun, Moon and/or Ascendant or Sun and/or Uranus rising or setting. This placing can often bring divorce or sudden terminations. Marriage may be regarded as being too restrictive or limiting and may be all together avoided. This is an excellent placing for astrologers as Uranus rules astrology and this house rules counseling and other people.

Eighth House: This personality is unconventional when it comes to physically expressing the romantic self. Intuition regarding the handling of other's finances is evident. Unorthodox views are likely expressed regarding matters of death, sex and the afterlife. Sudden financial gains or losses through others or unexpected sources are likely.

Ninth House: This native is intuitive and aspires to achieve higher knowledge. A meeting of the minds broadens intellectual horizons and motivates this personality. The intellect is progressive, original and independent from the conventional manner of thinking. Unusual learning habits, thoughts, ideas, beliefs and studies are likely to be of considerable interest. Unexpected situations are likely to arise while traveling abroad as well as encountering unusual people in foreign lands.

Tenth House: Original or unconventional methods or ideas are applied within the profession. Careers of interest include aviation, computer, engineering, radio and television. This placing often indicates work also involving electricity, astrology, astronomy, science, social work or humanitarian causes. Sudden changes or adjustments within the career are easily handled. This native works best alone when allowed to express creativity and independence. A reputation for being erratic or unstable may also arise.

Eleventh House: This personality demands freedom and unconventionality among friendships. Those selected are often eccentric, idealistic, or bohemian in nature. These friendships tend to form suddenly and end just as fast. There is something unusual about the relationships with friends as there is always some distance kept from them. Hopes and dreams can be shocking, unusual, or strange in some manner.

Twelfth House: Unusual, independent, or eccentric tendencies are likely suppressed. There is much intuition and mystery surrounding the persona. Dreams can be most insightful and inspiring. Attaining a high degree of spirituality would greatly benefit this native in order to counteract any fears or complexes and to balance the subconscious. This placing can also indicate an unusual or unconventional previous incarnation.

Empty Pisces Ascendant

This individual is emotional, sympathetic and intuitive. There is much creativity, imagination and intuition. The tendency toward self-deception, self-sacrifice, escapism, indecision, or over indulging should be controlled. The native should also avoid becoming easily swayed, tempted, or discouraged by others. Outer influences or environment have a strong effect upon the native's emotions and well-being as the tendency is toward being impressionable. Periods of seclusion are always welcomed due to an introverted disposition. This ascendant can project two different sides to the personality due to its dual nature. Or, another side of the personality may be hidden from others.

Neptune Through the Houses

Second House: Material comforts seem to contribute to a sense of self-worth. Creative and artistic work can bring financial security. Money is best earned through matters related to liquids, chemistry, photography, the sea, music, art, entertainment, charitable organizations, places of confinement and hospitals. There is also the ability to gain materially through intuition or gut feelings. Care should be taken with dubious deals as financial losses due to trickery, deceit, or misinformation is also evident.

Third House: This individual is not likely very talkative. The possibility of telling lies, or exaggerated truth, as well as being misinforming is also evident. The mind is highly impressionable and can be easily swayed. This placing indicates a high degree of intuition and imagination. It would be an excellent placing for a mystery or romance writer. Excessive day dreaming or worrying should be controlled.

Fourth House: Secretive or illusive issues surround the birth, childhood or family life. A need for an idealized domestic environment is strong however; there is the possibility of confusion, misunderstandings and possible deceptive conditions or events plaguing this area. A peaceful home life situated near water during the later years is likely.

Fifth House: The romantic life tends to somewhat idealized. This factor can cause much self-deception and vulnerability within such relationships, followed by disillusionments due to high expectations. The need for excessive fun or escaping from harsh realities through romantic relationships should be controlled. The personality is highly creative or artistic and is drawn to the theater, music, dance and art. Much care should be taken when speculating or gambling. It is very important for this native to express and release the abundance of creativity within.

Sixth House: This individual is able to tune into working conditions and co-workers. The job itself is often of a healing nature or within the service industry. Constantly being late or daydreaming while on the job can bring reversals. The tendency to be tricked or deceived by co-workers is also likely. Chances are that the native's work station is messy and unorganized. Health matters may be difficult to diagnose, however intuition can be very helpful here. Hygiene is very important for this native to maintain. Infections and setbacks due to drugs are to be monitored as super sensitivity to medication is evident.

Seventh House: This individual can idealize or be easily swayed by a spouse or partner. High expectations in this area can often result in disenchantment and disillusion. Extra caution should be taken to avoid misunderstandings and confusion within a marriage or partnership. The tendency toward self-sacrificing within this area is also evident. This placing often brings a spiritual soul mate. Compatibility with one born under Virgo or Pisces Sun, Moon and/or Ascendant as well as having Mercury and/or Neptune rising or setting is indicated.

Eighth House: Intuition is greatly enhanced with this placing. This native is highly imaginative and enjoys dreaming of idealized romantic encounters. Trickery or deception can be encountered through physically romantic experiences. When it comes to dealing with the finances of others, misunderstandings, dishonesty and confusion can bring reversals.

Ninth House: This placing enhances inspiration toward higher learning. The intellect is visionary and prophetic. Interest in foreign cultures and/or languages is indicated. The native projects an image of spirituality and exalted knowledge. Long distance travel brings a welcomed sense of escapism. This individual is drawn to life's mysteries as revelations are often experienced.

Tenth House: A career involving the arts, medicine and work of a spiritual nature is indicated. If cultivated properly, intuition can help the career. As a boss or employer, this individual can be sympathetic and understanding or dishonest and deceptive, depending upon aspects formed. This placing often brings misunderstandings with superiors. Other careers that can bring success include acting, bartending, dancing, fishing, photography, charitable or hospital work.

Eleventh House: This placing tends to attract friends of an artistic, spiritual, caring and compassionate nature. There is also the possibility of being tricked or deceived by unreliable friends or within questionable group associations. The native's hopes and dreams are highly idealistic. The tendency to daydream about these wishes provides a means of escape.

Twelfth House: This native possesses a wealth of intuition coupled with a powerful and hypersensitive subconscious mind. The need for secrecy, solitude and seclusion is strong. The tendency toward escapism and self-sacrifice should closely be monitored. This placing is often indicative of many secrets. Trickery or dishonesty can bring self-undoing.

Empty Second House

The second house answers questions involving financial and material goals, transactions and personal possessions. It also represents values, earning potential and wealth, gained or lost. The planetary ruler of this house when empty, is analyzed by the position and aspects formed to other planets. The aspects describe the potential or challenges within this department of life.

Empty Second House Aries

Spending habits are likely sudden or impulsive. Get rich quick schemes are often attracted. Much energy and initiative is expended in acquiring, earning and spending money. However, money can go just as easily as it comes. Financial setbacks or headaches may result from being too impatient or impulsive.

Mars is the ruler of this empty house. If found in the eleventh, impulsive spending with friends or within group organizations is indicated. Aggressive or adventurous friends are likely chosen. Financial status may depend upon or involve friendships or group efforts and organizations. The native believes that money can make dreams and wishes come true.

If Mars forms a trine with Neptune, self-control with finances is indicated. Money can be made through professions involving the sea, liquids, gases, photography, healing, dance, art and any form of creativity. Intuition can be applied to moneymaking ventures.

Empty Second House Taurus

This individual is able to save and does not hesitate to spend on quality and durability. There is a strong appreciation for the value of money and a frugal nature is not ruled out. Financial risks are seldom taken as the tendency is toward caution and practicality. On the other hand, this individual can also be most self-indulgent when it comes to spending on pleasures and luxuries.

Venus is the ruler of this empty house. If found in the sixth, jobs are never hard to find. This individual needs an attractive or pleasing work environment as well as harmonious relations with co-workers. The tendency to become involved in personal relationships with co-workers or finding romance through the workplace is indicated. Earning potential is best expressed through work or performing services for others. Self-worth comes from the job performed. The work itself may be related to beauty, health, or hygiene matters.

If Venus also forms a square with Jupiter, financial losses when dealing with foreign matters or individuals are indicated. Gambling should always be avoided as the tendency is toward being too confident or optimistic with money. Over-spending while traveling can also deplete the finances, affecting the health and/or working conditions. Weight gain from overindulging can bring serious health setbacks. Financial gains or losses may also be related to work and health matters.

Empty Second House Gemini

This individual is able to gain financially through communicative skills or abilities. This is a good placing for a financial speaker, advisor, or writer. Professions related to travel, lecturing, writing and teaching can also improve the financial outlook. Due to the duality of Gemini, finances can come from more than one source.

Mercury is the ruler of this empty house. If positioned in the eighth, numerous dealings or activities related to the finances of others are likely. Financial success can come through the management of other's money and resources. Occupations involving tax, refunds, legacies and inheritances can also further financial status.

If Mercury also forms a square with the Moon, financial losses or setbacks may arise from indecision or wrong decisions. Disputes are often experienced with females involving subjects such as occult matters, sex, death, or inheritances. Worrying over these matters or finances in general, can bring health problems. There are conflicts or challenges between the intellect and emotions. A calming attitude is recommended as the native can be somewhat high strung, nervous or anxious.

Empty Second House Cancer

This native enjoys spending money on the home and family. Financial gains or losses through a family member are indicated. Domestic and financial security is important to this individual. Business sense is sharp and intuition can bring financial gains. There is the tendency toward being highly protective of money and possessions. Clinging to material or financial wealth is likely however, due to the fluctuating nature of this sign, finances can also be unstable.

The Moon is the ruler of this empty house. If positioned in the first, personal efforts tend to be motivated by the chance to gain financially, as wealth is an important goal and motivating factor. Frequent changes within the financial status are likely to occur. Finances can increase through matters related to the Moon such as domestic products and services, hotel/restaurant work, healing, the food industry, real estate, or products related to water.

If the Moon forms an opposition with Jupiter, financial challenges and/or losses are likely to arise through dealings with partners, spouses, or open enemies. Entering into financial agreements with others should always be carefully analyzed. A separation, divorce, or lawsuit can prove to be very costly.

Empty Second House Leo

This individual enjoys spending money on glamorous and flashy items as appearance and self-worth are regarded as highly important issues. Others are often impressed by the native's extravagance and generosity. Creative abilities can enhance earning potential. A fondness for speculation or gambling is likely.

The Sun is the ruler of this empty house. If found in the tenth, financial goals motivate the career and professional ambitions. It is important for this individual to achieve some level of success, recognition, or prominence. Financial assistance may arise through contacts with older individuals, authority figures, or parent.

If the Sun also forms a square with Saturn, extra financial burdens may be experienced through a parent or older individual. The native may be forced to seriously consider financial limits at some time. Financial responsibilities may be put through the test through obstacles and challenges that can arise. Self-esteem or confidence may be lacking and disappointment or depression may result if these negative feelings are not altered.

Empty Second House Virgo

This individual can be frugal or careful with finances. The fear of poverty prevents gambling, speculation and reckless or careless spending. There is an element of shrewdness when it comes to handling financial matters as no detail, however small, can escape this personality. This is a good placing for a financial planner or analyst.

Mercury is the ruler of this empty house. If positioned in the seventh, financial and material acquisitions are gained through a marriage or partnership. It is very important for this native to have mental compatibility with the spouse or partner. Rapport or ideas combined and shared can bring financial rewards. This is a good placing for a financial advisor or counselor.

If Mercury also forms a conjunction with the Moon in the seventh house, the native can financially benefit through females or the mother. There is a good balance between the intellect and emotions and these faculties can be useful in financial dealings. Work involving real estate, hotel and restaurant industry, nursing, catering and domestic services can also bring monetary rewards.

Empty Second House Libra

This individual tends to spend on items of beauty and luxury, including trendy items and those of popular name brands. When it comes to handling money matters, this native is fair and just. Dealings with jewelry, fashion, luxury items, music and art can increase finances. Joint efforts and partnerships may bring financial rewards.

Venus is the ruler of this empty house. If found in the fifth, the individual spares no expense in living the good life, whether it is gambling, hobbies, dating, amusement, or recreational activities. Romantic partners tend to improve self-worth. These partners are often chosen for their financial or material security.

If Venus also forms a trine with Jupiter, romance and the luxuries in life are enjoyed to the fullest. This individual is generous, optimistic and popular. Material success can be expected, particularly through matters related to travel, hobbies, children, sports, law, languages, publishing, education and higher learning.

Empty Second House Scorpio

This native is resourceful and persistent when it comes to making money. There is a talent for transforming an idea or product in a money-making venture. Finances can also increase through areas involving death, investigation, research and secrecy. This placing often indicates hidden finances, shady, or secretive financial dealings.

Pluto is the ruler of this empty house. If positioned in the sixth, a talent for transforming and improving work methods is likely. As an employee, the personality is resourceful, determined and tireless. This native is not afraid to work hard to earn money and achieve financial and material security.

If Pluto also forms a trine with the Sun, financial benefits or assistance may come from a male co-worker or the father. Persistence, determination, investigation and research can bring monetary success. This individual must be in total control of finances and material possessions.

Empty Second House Sagittarius

This individual is generous with money and prone to over-spending. Learning to manage funds is important with this placing. Financial opportunities often arise and can involve foreign dealings, travel and higher learning. As hard as times may get, this personality never loses faith.

Jupiter is the ruler of this empty house. If found in the twelfth, the individual can expect karmic rewards for past life efforts. These rewards are likely to come in the form of financial and material acquisitions. Dealings with institutions such as hospitals and prisons, as well as within the field of psychology and counseling, can be financially rewarding. Secrecy and behind-the-scenes-activities often involve financial dealings.

If Jupiter also forms an opposition with Uranus, sudden financial changes can bring health setbacks. Speculation and gambling can bring heavy financial losses, and get rich quick schemes should always be avoided. Over confidence can bring financial obstacles and challenges. Learning to save and manage funds can relieve hard times.

Empty Second House Capricorn

This individual is most careful and economical with money. Purchases are based on durability and quality. Material and financial security is very important. Saving comes easily as the value of money is greatly appreciated. Investments are carefully scrutinized, as financial risks are seldom taken. Wealth can be achieved patiently through hard work and great effort.

Saturn is the ruler of this empty house. If found in the seventh, financial problems can cause delays or obstacles within a marriage or partnership. A late marriage can also affect the financial situation. Financial stability and security within these relationships is strongly required as there is a strong sense of responsibility and duty in this area. Life lessons revolve around marriage and partnerships, as well as material or financial goals and values.

If Saturn also forms a sextile with Venus, financial help may come from a spouse, partner, romantic interest, or females in general, as ruled by Venus. Finances are stable and opportunities often arise. Perseverance and determination are keys to acquiring wealth and fine possessions.

Empty Second House Aquarius

This individual possesses an unconventional approach when pursuing financial goals. Original and inventive ideas can bring wealth or financial opportunities. Unusual sources of income are likely as well as sudden or unexpected financial losses or windfalls.

Uranus is the planetary ruler of this empty house. If positioned in the third house, financial gains can be realized through communication, short distance travel, writing and teaching. Neighbors, siblings and same generation relatives can also influence finances.

If Uranus also forms an opposition with the Sun, financial losses through a male or the father can result. A high-strung or nervous temperament is likely, particularly when involved in discussions with siblings or same generation relatives. These arguments often involve money matters. Impulsiveness should be avoided when it comes to speculation and gambling with finances.

Empty Second House Pisces

This native possesses an evasive nature when it comes to earning and spending money. Extra caution should be applied when investing money, particularly with get-rich-quick schemes. Financial losses can come through deception, confusion, or mismanagement. There can be an element of secrecy surrounding money matters. Finances can improve through work involving art, dance, music, liquids, gases, photography, mysticism, psychic or charity work.

Neptune is the ruler of this empty house. If found in the ninth, finances can increase through publishing, law, travel, religion, spirituality, mysticism and higher education. Money can also be invested or made abroad. The knowledge of languages can increase wealth. Valuable financial tips can be received via intuition.

If Neptune also forms a square with Venus, a female, spouse, or partner can interfere with this native's earning potential. There is danger of being misled into deals that can produce losses. Escapist tendencies or activities can also deplete finances. All money matters, dubious or get-rich-quick schemes should be avoided or at least carefully investigated.

Second House Rulers

Regardless of the sign or ruling planet, we will briefly go through the ruler of the empty second house as it may be positioned throughout the remaining 11 houses. Always consider the aspects formed with this planet as it provides the necessary information as to determining whether these energies are beneficial or challenging.

The ruler of the empty second house found in the third shows financial benefits through connections with siblings, same generation relatives, neighbors, as well as with communicative skills. Teaching, writing and public speaking can be rewarding and may improve the financial status. Short distance travel, commuting and the transportation industry can also be financially successful.

The ruler of the empty second house found in the fourth indicates gains or losses through matters related to real estate, gardening, land, family and within the domestic industry. This individual does not hesitate in spending or investing within the home and property area. An inheritance from the parent represented by this house is likely.

The ruler of the empty second house found in the fifth reveals financial losses or gains through children, lovers, the entertainment industry, gambling, or speculation. This native enjoys spending money on fun activities and entertainment. A hobby can bring financial compensation.

The ruler of the empty second house found in the sixth increases motivation to earn through work or services performed for others. A job related to health, medicine, hygiene, or healing can bring financial gain. This placing often indicates work involving money, such as banking, investing, loans and financial advising or planning.

The ruler of the empty second house found in the seventh indicates that the native tends to experience financial gains or losses through partnerships or marriage. This is a fortunate placing for a financial advisor or consultant. Financial and material security is important to the marriage or partnership.

The ruler of the empty second house found in the eighth can bring benefits or losses through the spouse, partner, or the finances of others. Occupations involving tax, refunds, banks, legacies, inheritances and death are likely of interest.

The ruler of the empty second house found in the ninth brings financial gains or losses through higher education, law, religion, publishing, teaching, foreign dealings, languages and travel. Money can also be made, invested, or lost abroad.

The ruler of the empty second house found in the tenth indicates a substantial amount of money earned through the career and professional ambitions. Financial help can also come from an older individual, a parent, or one in a position of authority. It is important for this individual to project an air of wealth and prominence. An inheritance from the parent represented by this house is also likely.

The ruler of the empty second house found in the eleventh increases the likelihood of earning financially through group efforts and organizations. Friends can either help or hinder financial goals and dreams. The native's hopes and dreams involve financial and material luxuries and acquisitions.

The ruler of the empty second house found in the twelfth reveals a tendency toward financial gains or losses through institutions, secretive matters and psychological or subconscious issues. Money matters are kept private and secrets often surround the finances. Money can be made through behind the scenes activity. Karmic deeds can bring financial, rewards, opportunities, challenges, or losses.

The ruler of the empty second house found in the first indicates than wealth can be achieved or lost as a result of personal efforts. There is strong interest in financial or material acquisitions as much energy is expended in acquiring these goals. The native enjoys projecting an image of wealth and taste.

Empty Third House

The third house is studied when answers are sought to matters involving neighbors and immediate relatives of the same generation, such as siblings and cousins. Short distance travel, writing, communicative skills and learning abilities also fall under this house. The planetary ruler of this house when empty is analyzed by the position and aspects formed to other planets. The aspects describe the potential or challenges expected in this area of life.

Empty Third House Aries

This individual tends to be an abrupt, aggressive, quick or impulsive thinker or speaker. A short attention span coupled with a thrill or need to shock others with words is also indicative of this placing, particularly if Aquarius is rising. This native enjoys debates and will not back down from an argument. Relations with close relatives can be heated or quarrelsome.

Mars is the ruler of this empty house. If found in the first, the personality is outgoing and highly energetic. The manner of communication and thought tends to be aggressive and assertive. Learning to think before speaking can save a lot of grief or embarrassment. Frequent disagreements or arguments with siblings, neighbors and same age relatives are likely.

If Mars also forms a square with Uranus, impulsive ideas, hasty actions and decisions can bring setbacks, particularly among relationships with siblings, neighbors and same age relatives. If provoked, this native can display impatience, irritability and can even be somewhat combative. Short distance travel can be met with challenges or injuries, especially to the head as ruled by Aries.

Empty Third House Taurus

This individual takes time with thoughts and ideas that are carefully and methodically reached. Rarely does this native jump to conclusions. This is not the placing of a fast talker. Powers of concentration are well developed and words are carefully considered and selected. A resistance to change within the immediate environment, as ruled by this house, is evident.

Venus is the ruler of this empty house. If positioned in the fourth, a need for pleasant and peaceful communication within the home life or with the parent represented by this house is indicated. The home must be aesthetically pleasing surrounded by tasteful or artistic objects and furniture. There is much activity within the domestic area or circle.

Verbal skills and ideas can bring success in the fields of real estate, buildings, land, farming, housing, and the hotel and food industry.

If Venus also forms an opposition with Saturn, it may bring frequent arguments, responsibilities, restrictions, or challenges involving family members or a superior or boss. Emotional frustrations are also likely to involve siblings, same age relatives, neighbors and family in general. There is likely an inability to express warmth and affection to these family members.

Empty Third House Gemini

Gemini naturally rules this house and with this placing the native can be a natural speaker. The mind is restless, flexible, curious and changeable. The duality of Gemini suggests that several thoughts are able to occupy the mind at once. This individual expresses ideas and thoughts with ease and agility and is rarely at a loss for words. This is a versatile and fast talker who has a need for intellectual variety as boredom can easily set in. The powers of concentration may be somewhat deficient as the attention span can be sparse, particularly if fast Aries rises. A talent for public speaking, writing and/or teaching can be successfully developed. Much communication, gossip, or interchange of ideas with siblings and same age relatives are likely.

Mercury is the ruler of this empty house. If found in the twelfth, the person may enjoy being alone in seclusion with the multitude of thoughts and ideas that Mercury can deliver. This placing adds an element of shyness and compassion to the otherwise superficiality of Mercury. This can be an excellent placing for research and detective work. This individual knows how to ferret out secrets from others, particularly siblings and same generation relatives. This native can be trusted with secrets. There is the tendency to often speak with hidden meanings or mixed messages.

If Mercury also forms a trine with Neptune, this individual can be a wonderful dancer, writer, or actor as imagination is strong and well developed. The manner of speaking can captivate others. This would be an excellent placing for a counselor, public speaker, or storyteller as compassion and intellect are well integrated. This placing increases the level of intuition and the native may possess mediumistic abilities.

Empty Third House Cancer

This individual often takes a protective or parental role with siblings or same age relatives. Emotions and intuition play a large part in the thinking process. Changeable moods and thoughts are likely. The imagination may work overtime producing great storytellers or fantasy/fiction writers. Frequent short trips with family members are often taken and many short travels to visit relatives are also indicated. A good deed or hurt is never forgotten as an acute memory and retentive mind is indicated.

The Moon is the ruler of this empty house. If positioned in the fourth, the native enjoys conversing at home or with family members. This individual feels most secure when at home in a safe environment. There is a tendency to be overly protective of siblings and same age relatives. Much communication with the parent ruled by this house is indicated. Family disagreements can be highly emotional. These quarrels can best be worked out through talk and open communication; otherwise, domestic resentments can develop.

If the Moon also forms a sextile with Mercury, communication skills and mental faculties are well developed. This individual can excel as a speaker, teacher, writer, or family counselor. The intellect and emotions are harmoniously integrated. The memory and level of intuition is significantly above average. Much common sense is applied to decisions and choices. Many short distance travels are often taken.

Empty Third House Leo

This individual can be somewhat dramatic when communicating and expressing thoughts. The intellect is strong and fixed in opinion. A multitude of ideas are created and met with great energy and enthusiasm. As a profession, this individual can excel as a public speaker, teacher, or creative writer. Fun loving relationships with siblings and same age relatives are likely.

The Sun is the ruler of this empty house. If positioned in the sixth, a need to be appreciated and recognized at the workplace is strong. This native should avoid feelings of arrogance and excess pride as it may bring heated arguments to this area; otherwise, fun and friendly relations with co-workers are likely. Creative, communicative talents can bring many job opportunities as thoughts and ideas are best expressed in a working environment. Many short trips are likely experienced that are related to the job. In matters of health, as ruled by this house, care should be taken with the heart and back.

If the Sun also forms a trine with Neptune, creativity and imagination is strong and can be highly useful tools to use at work. Intuition is also enhanced and can be particularly insightful at work, with co-workers and for gaining insight into health matters. A career in healing, counseling, or the arts can also be rewarding.

Empty Third House Virgo

This personality is expressed in a most precise and articulate manner. Ideas are practical, logical and well thought out. The tendency to be critical of siblings and same age relatives should be controlled. Short trips are likely planned in such detail that there is little room for spontaneity that this sign tends to resist. The mind is detail-oriented, curious, studious and analytical. Facts are easily absorbed, as the individual is a quick learner.

Mercury is the ruler of this empty house. If found in the first, the personality is quick-witted and intellectual. There is no holding back in self-expression as the native enjoys being heard. This individual is highly active and most at ease when keeping busy. Many short distance travels and car trips are likely.

If Mercury also forms an opposition to Saturn, the native can be somewhat suspicious or defensive of others. It is especially important to cultivate feelings of honesty, optimism and cheerfulness. Communication with the spouse or partner can be blocked. Frequent arguments or disagreements with siblings are likely. Delays and/or misunderstandings can often arise while on short trips.

Empty Third House Libra

This individual communicates and expresses the mind in an elegant and refined manner. Rough or course language is not easily tolerated. Harmonious relations with siblings are likely. The mind is versatile, fair, honest and just. However, there can be a tendency toward difficulty in decision-making. The native can excel as a mediator due to being able to easily identify with both sides of issues. There is often interest or talent in the literary, artistic, musical, or any creative field.

Venus is the ruler of this empty house. If positioned in the ninth, foreign languages can easily be mastered as the native possesses verbal skills. This native highly enjoys exploring the mind through such topics as religion, philosophy, higher education, law and foreign cultures. Teaching, writing, publishing and law can be rewarding professions. Social or romantic connections can be made while abroad or encountered through institutions of learning. The spouse or partner is likely of foreign birth.

If Venus also forms a sextile with the Moon, the mind is highly receptive and imaginative. Communication can be most eloquent and refined. Good social relations can be maintained with siblings, females, family, foreigners and neighbors. This native is able to put others at ease with sympathetic or caring words.

Empty Third House Scorpio

This individual is most intellectually resourceful and creative. The mind is greatly influenced or clouded by emotions and extremes of opinions. A hurt or betrayal is never forgotten. Bluntness and/or sarcasm should be controlled, particularly with close relatives and neighbors. There is a talent for getting to the "bottom of things." Once the mind is made up it is not easily changed. Deep and penetrating thoughts are often expressed. Words should not be used to hurt or manipulate others.

Pluto is the ruler of this empty house. If it is found in the second, resourcefulness and intellectual tenacity can increase the financial outlook. Monetary gain or losses can be experienced through siblings or same generation relatives. Professions that can improve finances include writing, teaching, public speaking, literature and communication.

If Pluto also forms a trine with Mercury, the individual possesses astute intuitive faculties and powers of observation. This native is not easily fooled as the mind is probing, penetrating, resourceful, inquisitive and curious. This placing also favors researchers, detective work, financiers and bankers.

Empty Third House Sagittarius

This native is optimistic and possesses a great sense of humor and is highly capable of cheering people up. The personality is likely philosophic and the manner of speech can be blunt. This individual is restless and enjoys exploring or expanding intellectual horizons. There is interest in foreign languages that can be easily be mastered.

Jupiter is the ruler of this empty house. If found in the twelfth, the native enjoys being in solitude or escaping within the mind. The intellect is able to expand when spending time in solitude, seclusion, or introspection. This is an excellent placing for helping the less fortunate with compassionate words. Work involving social work, psychology, dream therapy, occult speaking or teaching can be most rewarding. Secrets are likely to involve siblings or same generation relatives. Older texts indicate that Jupiter in the twelfth house brings karmic and spiritual protection.

If Jupiter also forms a square with Mercury, the native is prone to exaggerate or being overly optimistic. Ideas are so grand that they are rarely followed through to completion. The tendency toward making big promises and bragging or boasting should be controlled. It is especially important for this individual to always be as honest as possible and to keep promises made to others in order to avoid secret troubles or enemies.

Empty Third House Capricorn

This individual is verbally reserved, a person of few words who says only what needs to be said. There is great capability for deep concentration. Powers of observation and logic are well developed. However, pessimism and depression can also manifest with this placing. Responsibilities through siblings or same generation relatives are likely as well as a sense of coldness or detachment to these relatives.

Saturn is the ruler of this empty house. If found in the seventh, marriage opportunities can be few or delayed. Communication problems may be the cause of these setbacks. Limited communication and lack of warmth within the marriage or partnership is likely.

There are karmic lessons to be learned through the marriage or partnership, particularly within the communication area. The spouse is often older or born under the sign of Capricorn.

If Saturn also forms a sextile with Jupiter, a successful partnership with a spouse, sibling or same age relative can manifest. Foreign contacts and travel with a spouse or partner can bring intellectual and spiritual benefits. Communication plays a vital role within these unions where mental compatibility and intellectual stimulation is crucial.

Empty Third House Aquarius

This individual is intellectually original and independent. The mind is curious, ingenious, clever and always open to new ideas and suggestions. Sudden flashes of inspiration are often felt. The manner of speech can be rapid, unpredictable and unique. The native often enjoys shocking others with innovative or unorthodox ideas and comments. Unusual or unexpected encounters while traveling short distance can be experienced. Siblings and same age relatives are often also considered as friends.

Uranus rules this house and is placed in the ninth. This individual often travels by air. Unusual encounters are to be expected while traveling as well as with foreigners. The mind is inventive, intuitive, progressive, independent and attracted to what is unorthodox and unconventional. Financial or personal gains can be achieved through communicative talents or ventures related to writing, advertising, publishing, education, transport, foreign relations, travel and law.

If Uranus also forms a trine with the Moon, unique thoughts and emotions are easily expressed. Intuition, originality and flashes of inspiration are often experienced. Good relations with siblings or same age relatives who live abroad are evident. Friendships, particularly those with females, are highly cherished.

Empty Third House Pisces

As Pisces is an introverted and often a shy sign, this may best describe the manner of communication. The intellect is highly influenced by emotions, intuition, imagination and compassion. Environment, other people and the weather can strongly influence this native's state of mind. Travel by water can be calming and healing. Feelings can easily be hidden from others and many secrets tend to be kept. Close ties with siblings and same generation relatives are evident. This placing is often found in the charts of the classic day dreamer; highly inspired by fantasy, romance, music, dance, art, poetry, cinema and the like. Psychic, musical, poetic or artistic talent is indicated.

Neptune is the ruler of this empty house. If found in the second, the finances can be increased or hindered through siblings or same age relatives. Ideas, manner of communication and intuition can be applied toward increasing finances. Wealth can be best achieved through ventures related to water, liquids, gasses, the sea, medicine, clairvoyance and all manner of communication. This placing suggests avoiding dubious or questionable financial schemes as losses can result through deception or fraud.

If Neptune also forms a conjunction to the Sun, the native inherits traits of Pisces. This individual tends to communicate in an evasive or unclear manner. Intuitive faculties are strengthened, however there is danger of self-delusion or vagueness. It is important for this individual to be as honest with others as possible, particularly to siblings and when involved with financial deals and transactions. Behind the scenes methods can be applied toward financials goals.

Third House Rulers

Regardless of the sign or ruling planet, we will briefly go through the ruler of the empty third house as it may be positioned throughout the remaining 11 houses. Always consider the aspects formed with this planet as they provide the necessary information as to determining whether these planetary energies are beneficial or challenging.

The ruler of the empty third house found in the fourth indicates that there is much activity within the home and domestic area. Communication within the family is frequent and highly important. Verbal skills can best be applied to such professions involving real estate, land, building, architecture, farming, housing and the domestic, hotel or food industry.

The ruler of the empty third house found in the fifth brings intellectual creativity and ability to win at contests requiring mental skill. Hobbies tend to involve or challenge the mind. There is ability to easily relate to children. Communicating with siblings, same generation relatives and romantic partners are essential. This is a good placing for a stand up comedian or a sports commentator.

The ruler of the empty third house found in the sixth increases communicative skills. Friendly relations with co-workers are evident. A job that challenges the mind or requires the expression of ideas can bring rewards. Conversations with co-workers or office gossip can be of particular interest. Working with a sibling or same age relative is likely. Additional jobs that are also suited include writing, teaching and public speaking. Short trips are often experienced with co-workers or for reasons related to the job.

The ruler of the empty third house found in the seventh reveals that communication and intellectual compatibility are vital to the marriage or partnership. The spouse or partner must be active, witty and communicative. A partnership may be formed with a sibling, same generation relative or neighbor.

The ruler of the empty third house found in the eighth shows that communicative skills can become an asset when handling finances earned or gained through others, such as loans, taxes or inheritances. The native is curious about sex, death and the afterlife.

The ruler of the empty third house found in the ninth indicates that frequent travels and the pursuit of education are regarded as important goals. This is a good placing for work related to publishing, advertising, teaching, foreign dealings, travel, religion, law and writing. The desire and ability to master foreign languages is likely.

The ruler of the empty third house found in the tenth brings frequent important communication with a parent, boss or higher authority individuals. The career must provide an outlet for the intellect and creative skills. Siblings and same generation relatives can help or hinder the career and reputation. This is a good position for a writer or public speaker.

The ruler of the empty third house found in the eleventh indicates that close relatives and siblings are considered as friends. However, these friends can either help or hinder the native's hopes and dreams. The friends that are chosen must provide much intellectual compatibility, rapport and stimulation. This is a good placing for a speaker within group organizations.

The ruler of the empty third house found in the twelfth reveals a highly active subconscious mind. This is a good placing for a psychologist, researcher, writer, teacher or speaker of the occult. Secrets involving siblings are often present with this placing. The native may be shy, secretive and introspective. Periods of seclusion are often sought where the native can spend quality time in solitude with thoughts and ideas.

The ruler of the empty third house found in the first shows an enthusiastic and highly communicative individual. Self-expression is seldom held back as the personality is talkative and witty. Thoughts are easily communicated to others, especially to siblings and same generation relatives. This individual is active, enjoys keeping busy and frequently takes short trips.

The ruler of the empty third house found in the second indicates that financial gains or losses are likely experienced through siblings or same age relatives. Financial earnings can increase through writing, teaching or any profession requiring mental skills.

Empty Fourth House

The fourth house answers questions involving the home and domestic environment, childhood issues, property, land, real estate, heredity, emotional responses from childhood responses, conditions late in life, family and the parent represented by this house. The planetary ruler of this house when empty, is analyzed by the position and aspects formed to other planets. The aspects describe the potential or challenges within this department of life.

To determine which parent is ruled by this house, many factors need to be considered. Texts seldom agree upon which house rules which parent. In Nicholas Devore's *Encyclopedia of Astrology* the following theories regarding the rulership of the tenth house are presented; therefore the opposite house being the fourth, rules the other parent.

The tenth house rules:

- the father
- the father in a female chart
- the mother in a day birth
- the parent of the same sex as the native
- the parent with more influence

Through extensive research, I have come to the conclusion that the fourth and tenth house rulership over the parents differs within charts. That is to say, that the same rule does not always apply to all charts. As each chart is unique and individual, so is the determination of the parent ruled by the fourth and tenth houses. One individual may have the fourth house representing the mother while another has the mother being represented by the tenth house.

The parent is not individualized by either house specifically, but through the planetary and sign placings therein. As there is always a strong connection or link through the chart of the child to the parents and vice versa, we look to compare the Sun, Moon and Ascendant sign of each parent to the conditions of the child's fourth and tenth house.

My parents are clearly individualized through my chart. My father was born under a Pisces Sun. Neptune, ruler of Pisces, is the most elevated (closest to the Midheaven) planet in my chart. He is a well-known artist who teaches and is often in the public eye as represented by the Midheaven.

Therefore, the fourth house represents my mother. This must not be assumed but proven. Her Moon is in Aries, disposited by Mars. Mars forms a conjunction to my fourth house. Of interest is that her mother (my grandmother) was born under an Aries Sun.

To confirm the above, the Sun, as we know, rules the father and the Moon rules the mother. My Sun sign is Leo, which is my father's rising sign. My Moon is in Virgo, which is my mother's rising sign. Fortunately, I have planets forming a conjunction with the IC and Midheaven, making it easier to determine which parent is represented by these houses.

Should these houses be empty, we take the rulers of these cusps and analyze them. If more than one planet is found in both or either house, look to a combination or blend of these planets. Consider the planet closest to the cusp of the fourth and tenth house for greatest influence.

Empty Fourth House Aries

Arguments and quarrels within the domestic circle are likely. When it comes to dealing with family or domestic issues, the manner can be aggressive, impulsive, competitive or enthusiastic. Many changes of residence are evident as boredom and the need to explore often arises. Much energy is spent at home and accidents should be avoided in this area. This individual must be the leader of the household otherwise arguments or conflicts may arise.

Mars is the ruler of this empty house. If found in the second, much aggression, extravagance, initiative or activity regarding the acquisition of finances and/or material possessions is evident. Hasty financial discussions and decisions should be avoided in order to prevent monetary setbacks or losses. Impulsive spending when it comes to the home can be a problem as money may easily come and go. Self-worth is often measured by the conditions in the home life with this placing. Family ties may affect the finances and inheritances are not ruled out.

If Mars also forms a square with Uranus, the native should watch for accidents or fire in the home. Recklessness or taking risks with finances can cause domestic losses. Quick decisions or hasty actions taken within the home life or regarding a relative can bring monetary setbacks. Financial problems due to impulsiveness can lead to arguments and domestic losses.

Empty Fourth House Taurus

A need for an aesthetically pleasing and peaceful, comfortable, stable and luxurious home environment is indicated. This individual is loyal and reliable when it comes to family matters. There is great affection and/or attachment to the birthplace or the parent ruled by this house. The native does not hesitate when spending money in order to enhance the home environment. As Taurus is the sign of money, financial gain or an inheritance may come from a parent or family member.

Venus is the ruler of this empty house. If found in the ninth, an interest or fondness for foreign cultures, music and the arts is often enjoyed from the home. This is an ideal placing for teaching from the home. Much time far away from the family and/or place of birth is likely experienced as a residence may be established abroad or in a foreign land. The latter part of life will likely be lived in such a place.

If Venus also forms a trine with Uranus, this individual is highly creative and innovative. There is an element of independence and unpredictability within the family circle. Family members that live abroad are fondly remembered. Unusual or sudden contacts could bring financial or romantic benefits as ruled by Venus. Artistic talent expressed from the home can be successful. Foreign contacts and friends are welcomed within the home and family circle. Sudden good fortune is likely to come through domestic ties, land or real estate dealings, perhaps in a foreign land.

Empty Fourth House Gemini

There is a strong indication of owning two homes at once or experiencing frequent changes of residence. A well-stocked library or collection of books is often kept in the home. Much communication with family members is evident. This native can spend hours at home on the telephone talking to relatives. An active and busy home life is likely.

Mercury is the ruler of this empty house. If positioned in the tenth, family status and reputation is important. With this placing, it becomes harder to distinguish one parent from the other within the native's chart. In this example, the native's mother has a Virgo Sun and is represented by Mercury in the tenth house. The native's father has Gemini rising as indicated by Gemini ruling the empty fourth house.

If Mercury also forms a trine with Pluto, will power, level of understanding and concentration are pronounced, particularly within the family and career area. Creative or intellectual ideas created from the home can further reputation and career ambitions. This is an ideal placing for work involving writing, research and investigation. This individual is seldom fooled or deceived by others, particularly family members or superiors.

Empty Fourth House Cancer

Strong family ties are evident as well as deep emotional satisfaction or attachment with relatives and within the domestic circle. Family traditions are upheld and childhood memories fondly remembered. The individual is interested in family roots and ancestral history. This native is protective, dedicated and sympathetic to family and loved one's needs. Domestic security is important, as the home is a refuge. At some point, particularly during the later years as ruled by this house, a home by water is indicated.

The Moon is the ruler of this empty house. If found in the fifth, the individual is likely quite fond of children and will probably have several. A close bond with offspring and family is indicated. Romantic relationships are largely based on emotional needs. Creative ideas and inspiration are best expressed at home, perhaps as a hobby.

If the Moon also forms an opposition with Mercury in the eleventh house, friends and group ties can obstruct or interfere within the native's romantic pursuits or family life. There can be a lack of communication or confusion among family members, friends or romantic partners resulting in emotional quarrels. Excess worry over the home life, romantic life and friendships should be minimized.

Empty Fourth House Leo

This native is proud of the home, family and roots. The home itself is likely decorated in fine and expensive tastes where guests are often entertained. The grandness and generosity of Leo in this house can bring difficulties in remaining within budget for domestic purchases and needs. Domestic security is important, as is a happy home where the individual is the king or queen of the castle.

The Sun is the ruler of this empty house. If found in the ninth, the native is likely to either move abroad or have a second home in a foreign land far from the place of birth. Studying, teaching and meditating from the home can bring spiritual benefits. The individuality is best expressed through higher learning and expanding mental horizons. There is a need to be free and independent, to explore and roam, whether physically or mentally.

If the Sun also forms a trine with Neptune, emotions and creativity are best expressed through art, dance, music or spirituality. Mental and spiritual benefits can also arise by spending time at home in seclusion expanding the intellect, exploring intuition or the highly creative potential. Long journeys can be successful and enlightening. Foreign décor or objects from other cultures likely beautify the home, which can be most rewarding when situated near water.

Empty Fourth House Virgo

This individual prefers an orderly and neat home, as there is a tendency toward being fussy and meticulous about how the home is kept and run. Fault-finding and being over-analytical with a parent or immediate family member is evident. Family health is important to the native. The early years or childhood may have been lacking in warmth. Emotions may be over-analyzed and picked apart. This placing often indicates work performed from the home.

Mercury is the ruler of this empty house. If positioned in the third, gains from studies, writing, communication or sales related to domestic products or services, real estate or property dealings are likely. This is a good placing for an author who writes from the home. Relationships to siblings or relatives of the same generation can be somewhat superficial however; witty conversations and exchanging ideas with these relatives are greatly enjoyed.

If Mercury also forms a square with Mars, the manner of speech can be abrupt and often provokes others. This native may experience frequent arguments or differences of opinions with a parent, close relative or sibling. The tendency toward being headstrong, sarcastic or impulsive should strongly be avoided. Many family problems can be minimized by slowly thinking things through first and not jumping to conclusions as the mind has a tendency to do so.

Empty Fourth House Libra

This individual possesses a tendency toward being somewhat judgmental of a parent or the family; however, peace at all costs is desired. The home must project an image of balance and elegance with aesthetically pleasing items and furniture. Balance in domestic matters is imperative, as the home environment must consist of emotional stability, sociability and artistry. The native can also be somewhat indecisive in domestic matters due to the ability to see both sides to family issues.

Venus rules this empty house. If found in the first, a pleasant manner and attractive appearance is likely as Venus here bestows beauty. The personality is best expressed through domestic issues, which are of utmost importance as the family environment has a strong hold on the native. The home is often used for artistic or social gatherings. Family roots and birthplace are fondly remembered, particularly in later years.

If Venus also forms a conjunction with Neptune, a career requiring creativity, intuition and inspiration can bring success. An interior home decorator would be an appropriate choice. Objects of elegance and fine taste often decorate the home base. Imagination and artistic creativity is strong and can best be expressed through family matters. There is great sensitivity and intuition regarding the opinion of others as well as in matters of the heart. A home by water can bring spiritual and/or financial rewards.

Empty Fourth House Scorpio

This native is highly protective or secretive regarding the family life. There is a tendency to be somewhat suspicious of relative's motives or actions. The individual can be reserved and quiet as well as possessive and manipulative with family members. Domestic roots and emotional ties are strong and deep. This placing often brings a family inheritance late in life.

Pluto rules this empty house. If positioned in the seventh, an emotionally or sexually intense relationship with the spouse or partner is likely. The spouse may be met through family related connections or may be a reflection of the parent ruled by the fourth house. Personal transformations and growth can be experienced within the marriage or domestic life. Marriage or leaving home to move in with another can come early, as the native does not enjoy living alone.

If Pluto also forms a square with Mars, power struggles, arguments, suspicions, secrets and trouble can plague the domestic environment, the marriage or partnership. An intensely emotional nature and domineering attitude should be avoided particularly with relatives, spouses or partners.

Empty Fourth House Sagittarius

This individual is generous, extravagant and optimistic within the domestic circle. A big family is likely, however much space is required within the home environment. Property in a foreign land, as ruled by this house, can be most joyful, fortunate and rewarding, particularly during the golden years.

Jupiter is the ruler of this empty house. If found in the eleventh, the native often enjoys entertaining friends at home. Family members are regarded as friends. This individual has many friends and some go back to childhood. There is a tendency toward being too generous or overly optimistic with friends and family members. This placing indicates frequent travels with relatives and friends.

If Jupiter also forms a trine with the Moon, an inheritance from a friend, relative or the mother can come late in life, resulting in a greatly improved home life. Domestic relations are open, optimistic and fun loving. Matters involving land or real estate can bring success, particularly if near water. Devotion to friends and family is pronounced, especially with female members.

Empty Fourth House Capricorn

This individual prefers a well-kept and organized home environment. The childhood was likely strict and family or domestic relations may be lacking in warmth, affection or closeness. Much responsibility is likely to arise from a parent or within the family. It is important for the domestic environment to project an image of success or social standing. However, little socializing is actually experienced at the home as it is regarded as a private haven. Tradition and roots within the family are important. Often, there is a marked interest in ancestry such as researching the family tree with this position.

Saturn is the ruler of this empty house. If found in the twelfth, the tendency is toward having family secrets and restrictions imposed upon by domestic relations or situations. The native will likely become a recluse in later years, as domestic privacy is important.

This placing reveals that the individual's karma is the home life. Fears, sorrows, and limitations are likely self-imposed, particularly those involving childhood, the parents, close relatives or within family and home environment. This is a good placing for caring for the elderly.

If Saturn also forms an opposition with the Sun, a very strict parent may have greatly influenced this individual. Restrictions within the family circle are likely to arise from the father or parent represented by the tenth house. Emotions are not easily expressed to parents, relatives or peers and particularly to those that are male. Domestic ties or responsibilities may impede or interfere with the native's career goals or public standing, or the career itself somehow hinders the family life. It is important for this individual to cultivate feelings of self-worth and self-love.

Empty Fourth House Aquarius

This individual is attracted to an unusual domestic environment and relations. Unexpected experiences are often encountered involving relatives and family life. The home is likely equipped with many electronic devices or appliances and computers. Family members are also friends; however, there is some distance kept due to the independent nature of this sign. The native's upbringing may have been unusual or unconventional in some manner as this placing indicates an unstable home life during childhood.

Uranus rules this empty house. If positioned in the eleventh, close family members and friends are often entertained or welcomed in the home. The friendships that are formed tend to be with eccentric, unusual or bohemian-like individuals. The native's hopes and dreams are centered on the domestic environment, family life and close friendships. This placing tends to bring many childhood friends throughout the lifetime.

If Uranus also forms a sextile with Mercury, chances of these hopes and dreams are increased through conversations and ideas shared with friends or family members as well as with the parent ruled by this house. The individual is self-reliant, intelligent, and independent of family and friends. Unusual, original, or innovative ideas and many conversations can be shared among friends and family members. Traveling with friends or family can be rewarding.

Empty Fourth House Pisces

This individual experiences strong and emotional family ties, however due to the flexibility of this sign, these relationships are also fluctuating and inconstant. There is an element of self-sacrifice involving relations with the parent ruled by this house, a relative, or within the domestic circle. The home must be a safe and protective refuge where much time can be spent in seclusion exploring the creative expression. A home by water at some point in life will bring peace and happiness.

Neptune is the ruler of this empty house. If found in the eighth, the individual possesses psychic abilities. Peculiar dreams are often experienced due to a highly receptive nature. Secrets, deceptive conditions or misinterpretations may involve family members as well as property or land dealings, joint resources or the parent ruled by this house. Finances may be affected by owning property by water. There is a strong possibility of receiving a family inheritance in the form of property or land by water.

If Neptune also forms a square with Mars, a home by water would not be the wisest choice to consider. Avoid becoming involved in financial transactions with family members. Much preventative caution should be taken to avoid accidents with sharp objects or poisoning of some sort, particularly while at home. Childhood issues may conflict with psychological issues. Secrets involving the family life tend to bring frequent arguments; particularly with the parent ruled by this house. This individual is highly sensitive to family issues.

Fourth House Rulers

Regardless of the sign or ruling planet, we will briefly go through the ruler of the empty sixth house as it may be positioned throughout the remaining 11 houses. Always consider the aspects formed with this planet as it provides the necessary information as to determining whether these energies are beneficial or challenging.

The ruler of the empty fourth house found in the fifth shows that creative expression is best expressed at home, through a hobby or with matters involving children. The home is often filled with young people and children, as strong ties are evident. Games, fun and entertainment are often experienced at home or with family members. This native can be emotional or needy when it comes to romance.

The ruler of the empty fourth house found in the sixth indicates that this native's home is neatly kept, clean and organized. Pets are likely a big part of the family. This individual is best suited to working at home or in industries related to domestic products, services or the health industry. Further career options include the food, hotel, land and real estate industry.

The ruler of the empty fourth house found in the seventh reveals that this individual does not enjoy living alone and an early marriage will likely result. The native will never be short of a roommate, whether spouse, partner or friend. The domestic life of the marriage or partnership is very important and must be solid. The spouse or partner may possess similar attributes to the parent ruled by the fourth house.

The ruler of the empty fourth house found in the eighth brings the strong possibility of receiving a family inheritance in the form of land or property. Secrets and suspicions within the domestic environment are likely. Financial matters involving property deeds, insurance, wills and taxes can play an important role. The end of life may come late and peacefully at home.

The ruler of the empty fourth house found in the ninth shows that a home is preferred abroad or in a foreign land. The latter part of life will likely be spent in a distant country. This placing tends to bring benefits through foreign land or property dealings as well as work involving tutoring, teaching and studying from the home.

The ruler of the empty fourth house found in the tenth indicates that close relations with a parent or parents are likely. Their approval and advice is highly considered. The career and family life are somehow at odds with each other. It is important to project a solid family background and high social standing within the community.

The ruler of the empty fourth house found in the eleventh reveals that friends are considered as family, and family members are also regarded as friends. These people are often entertained and welcomed in the home. Friends, organizations and social alliances can further the native's hopes and dreams, which often center on family issues and domestic bliss. Childhood friends may last a lifetime.

The ruler of the empty fourth house found in the twelfth indicates that the individual enjoys and requires frequent periods of introspection at home, particularly during the latter years when the native may become somewhat of a recluse. The childhood, the parent ruled by this house or family member may be a source of secrets and sorrows. The native's karma is family and the home life.

The ruler of the empty fourth house found in the first reveals that the home environment is of the utmost importance to the native. It is with relatives, family or the parent ruled by this house that the personality is best expressed. This individual strives for domestic happiness and a successful and healthy family life.

The ruler of the empty fourth house found in the second shows that a family member or the parent ruled by this house may further the native's financial goals. Finances are often tied to domestic products, the hotel, land, real estate or food industry. The home base must be aesthetic, comfortable, solid and secure.

The ruler of the empty fourth house found in the third can bring success through writing, communicating or studying from the home. Short distance travel involving sales of products, particularly domestic items, can also be successful. Frequent commuting between home and work is likely experienced with this placing. There is much communication with family members, particularly siblings and same generation relatives as well as the parent ruled by this house.

Empty Fifth House

The fifth house answers questions involving children, hobbies, lovers and romance. It also represents creative expression, early schooling environment, entertainment, holidays, gambling, games, hobbies and sports. The planetary ruler of this house when empty, is analyzed by the position and aspects formed to other planets. These aspects describe the potential or challenges within this department of life.

Empty Fifth House Aries

This individual tends to be somewhat aggressive and enthusiastic when it comes to matters of the heart and speculation. In both these areas, impulsive decision-making should be avoided. Within romantic relationships, the native enjoys the chase and there is no hesitation in making first moves. A short temper and impatience with children should be controlled. This placing tends to bring a love of sports and competition. Creative inspiration may quickly come and go.

Mars is the ruler of this empty house. If found in the second, the tendency toward being financially impulsive, ambitious or aggressive is heightened. Earning ability is well developed. Financial gain may be achieved through creative outlets and hobbies. Excessive gambling may become a problem if not controlled. In romance, entertaining and handling children, the native can be most generous.

If Mars also forms a trine with the Sun, much energy is expended in furthering personal romantic or financial goals. Traits of self-confidence, generosity and assertiveness are increased. Good relations with children are evident and this would be a good placing for teaching as the Sun rules Leo, the fifth house traditionally while representing children. This individual can be lucky in romantic or financial matters under fortunate transits or progressions.

Empty Fifth House Taurus

This native is patient, reliable, loyal and persistent, particularly with children and matters related to romance. There is little attraction to gambling, as the tendency to avoid taking chances with finances and romance is likely. There is a strong appreciation for beauty, art and music as well as fondness for children and romantic partners.

Venus is the ruler of this empty house. If positioned in the fourth, the domestic environment must be comfortable, secure and visibly appealing as aesthetic objects are appreciated. This position can indicate inheritance received from the parent ruled by this empty house.

There are also strong emotional ties to this parent or the family in general. Romantic partners are often entertained at home. Artistic flair is likely and is often expressed as a hobby, such as gardening or cooking. This is also a good placing for an interior decorator. Good relationships with offspring are likely, particularly the first-born.

If Venus also forms a square with Jupiter, overspending in luxurious possessions for the home is likely. Spoiling or over-indulging romantic partners and children are also evident. This aspect brings an abundance of romantic relationships and over-expectations in this area should be avoided as difficulties and disappointments may arise.

Empty Fifth House Gemini

This individual enjoys communicating with children and has a certain popular way with them as they are dealt with on an intellectual level. The chance of having twins with this position is slightly higher than average although other factors in the chart need to be analyzed. Mental games and intellectual pursuits or hobbies are often of interest. Romantic partners tend to be younger in age. More than one relationship at a time is indicated due to the duality of this sign in the house of romance. Variety, conversation, verbal and intellectual compatibility in romantic relationships are essential to prevent them from becoming stagnant.

Mercury is the ruler of this empty house. If found in the eleventh, many friends and acquaintances of a younger, literary or intellectual type are maintained. There is a deep appreciation for the exchange of ideas and communication with friends or in clubs and group organizations. Traveling with friends, lovers and children can be highly rewarding.

If Mercury also forms a square with Neptune, there is danger of being influenced or misguided by lovers, friends or children. Schemes and deception of all kinds should be avoided. A strong imagination can bring setbacks if not controlled. It is important to be clear and honest in conversations and dealings with lovers, friends as well as children. It is also important not to trust a friend or romantic potential completely until sure of their sincerity as unrealistic expectations can get in the way of happy relationships.

Empty Fifth House Cancer

This individual is most receptive and caring when it comes to handling children and romantic partners. This is a fruitful placing for having children. Past lovers are often remembered throughout life. The tendency toward being overly possessive, protective and highly emotional should be controlled particularly with children and romantic partners. When it comes to romances, there can be an element of inconsistency. The potential for creativity is great as imagination is powerful. This native is somewhat intuitive when it comes to understanding children and lovers.

The Moon is the ruler of this empty house. If found in the third, a fertile and inquisitive imagination is coupled with writing skills and strong communicative abilities. The desire for learning and expressing creativity is strong. Many short distance travels are likely as this individual is restless and tends to bore easily. A protective role is often taken with siblings.

If the Moon also forms a square with Uranus, erratic emotions can influence reason or thinking. Moods can be changeable and often vary unexpectedly. Impulsive or nervous behavior can bring losses, particularly in relations involving the mother, children, siblings or romantic partners. An unusual or offbeat quality about the mother or within the relationship is likely.

Empty Fifth House Leo

This individual is quite fond of fun, children, entertainment, sports, and games. A love of romance brings many such relationships. There is a high level of creativity, generosity and enthusiasm that can be contagious to others. Children are none or few unless other factors contradict. Teaching or working with children as well as any creative outlet can bring personal success.

The Sun is the ruler of this empty house. If positioned in the tenth, the native can make a successful career in work involving creativity, children, sports and the entertainment industry. The drive and desire for achievement is strong and motivated by the need to project a successful image to the world. The closer the Sun is positioned to the Midheaven, the better the chances of success.

If the Sun also forms a trine with Jupiter, an abundance of creativity, generosity and optimism is indicated. Many children are likely as Jupiter brings abundance. Financial speculation can bring profits and professional status or achievements may increase wealth. Social and professional life is healthy as the individual is highly popular in all circles.

Empty Fifth House Virgo

This individual is somewhat reserved and introverted. Creative talents and hobbies are inclined to be of an intellectual nature, such as writing and studying. Emotions and romantic issues are constantly analyzed as perfectionist tendencies in this area are indicated. Being over-critical of romantic partners and children should always be controlled.

Mercury is the ruler of this empty house. If found in the ninth, emphasis is on furthering education. The mind is alert, exploring, inquisitive, adaptable and literary. Opportunities for travel may provide intellectual advancement and introduce romantic encounters or potentials. Short-term relationships tend to be formed with foreigners or those met abroad. This placing tends to show interest in the study of foreign languages. Teaching, law, spirituality, philosophy and publishing can also be rewarding outlets or careers.

If Mercury also forms a sextile with the Moon, worthwhile opportunities for travel or advancing education may arise through the mother or females in general. Traveling with children or romantic partners can be rewarding. Memory is strong and the mind is receptive and intuitive. The emotions are well integrated with the intellect.

Empty Fifth House Libra

This individual is highly creative and has a strong appreciation and need for romantic activity. The concept of love and romance however, is most ideal as expectations are high in this area. Personality is sociable, fair-minded but somewhat indecisive when it comes to handling children and romantic relationships. Communication is best expressed with children and lovers on an intellectual rather than emotional level. There is a strong appreciation for beauty, aesthetics and items of luxury.

Venus is the ruler of this empty house, if positioned in the second; the finances are strongly affected by children, romantic partners and short-term relationships, hobbies or entertainment. There is a tendency to spend money on luxury items such as art, fashion or jewelry. Creative talents can bring financial success. The tendency to gamble can also affect finances.

If Venus also forms a square with Pluto, a love of power, luxury and extravagance is evident. Relationships may suffer due to financial disagreements or troubles. Romance can also become a source of financial drain or loss. This individual will not be controlled or overpowered by romantic partners. The tendency to control or dominate within these relationships should be avoided. There can be an attraction to secret love affairs.

Empty Fifth House Scorpio

This individual tends to be somewhat emotionally intense, particularly when dealing with children and romantic partners. Power struggles and jealousy should be avoided or controlled within these relationships. There is great energy, passion and determination when pursuing romance or creative interests. When it comes to sports and games, the native possesses much stamina and courage. Secrecy often involves children or romantic partners.

Pluto is the ruler of this empty house. If found in the third, the tendency to dominate siblings, lovers or children is likely. The mind is penetrating yet powerfully creative, intuitive and somewhat suspicious, especially of siblings and romantic partners. Secrecy may also involve a sibling or same generation relative. This is a good placing for writing children's books, particularly mysteries.

If Pluto also forms an opposition with the Moon, the emotional nature can be suspicious, jealous, possessive and can even be somewhat sarcastic when dealing with children, romantic partners, siblings and the mother or females in general. There may be a control issue with the mother or a female regarding children or romance. Siblings or children can also interfere with the native's personal relationships and pursuit of fun and entertainment. Mood swings are likely and feelings can be deeply hurt if affections are not returned.

Empty Fifth House Sagittarius

This individual is outgoing, fun loving and optimistic. Interest in sports, games, the outdoors and gambling is likely. In romantic relationships, there must be a certain amount of freedom allowed due to a need for independence, excitement and adventure in this area. This native is often lucky in romance, as many opportunities tend to arise. Many children are also likely when this sign of abundance is placed here.

Jupiter is the ruler of this empty house. If positioned in the sixth, good health and many opportunities for work are indicated. Employment of a creative nature or working with children can bring most success. Good relations with co-workers or employees are indicated.

If Jupiter also forms a square with Mercury, mental laziness at the workplace can often be experienced. Much caution should be taken in order to have all the correct facts before speaking at the workplace or with co-workers so as to avoid arguments. This native would do best to avoid impulsive judgment and decision making in this. Over-confidence at the workplace or with children will not bring the best results.

Empty Fifth House Capricorn

This native can be somewhat emotionally distant or creatively challenged. Much caution is exercised when it comes to matters of the heart. When dealing with children and romantic partners, a cold or undemonstrative nature is evident. Romantic partners tend to be of a difference in age. Children can be few and may bring many responsibilities. Interest in hobbies or games that require determination, patience, concentration and effort tend to be of most interest. This individual rarely takes chances with finances and romance.

Saturn is the ruler of this empty house. If found in the ninth, the intellect is serious, deep and thoughtful. Patience, hard work and a traditional approach is taken when pursuing education and expanding the intellect. Romantic partners are often foreigners or met while abroad. Connections to older individuals from distant lands are also indicated. The native is likely attracted to teaching, publishing, law and pursuing higher knowledge.

If Saturn also forms a square with Pluto, delays and losses may occur as a result of dealing with foreigners or while in a distant land that can bring legal trouble. This placing does not bestow many children unless several other factors contradict. Power struggles with foreigners, children and romantic partners should strongly be avoided.

Empty Fifth House Aquarius

This individual can be emotionally independent, unpredictable, friendly and highly sociable. Romantic partners often develop from friendships, and lovers tend to remain as friends. Sudden or unusual romances are often attracted, particularly to intellectual or bohemian types. There is a need for independence and experimentation within personal relationships. The native tends to relate best to romantic partners and children on an intellectual rather than emotional level. Children can also be a good source of friendship.

Uranus is the ruler of this empty house. If positioned in the seventh, sudden, unusual or unconventional conditions continue into the marriage or long-term relationship. Friends and lovers may turn into rivals or competitors. Children are an important factor within the marriage or partnership. This placing tends to bring many opportunities for love at first sight.

If Uranus also forms an opposition with Venus rising in the first house, the chances of legal or marital trouble are increased. A romance on the side can bring losses to a marriage or partnership, perhaps even affecting the children. Unusual or distant relationships with children are likely. This placing increases the need for independence and personal freedom. It is important for this individual to learn social discretion as well as how to meet others halfway.

Empty Fifth House Pisces

This individual is highly imaginative, emotional and creative. Emotions can also be changeable due to the fluctuating nature of this sign. A great love of children, romance and fantasy is likely; a true romantic at heart. Secret relationships are often of interest and like hobbies and expressing creativity, provide a great source of escapism. This individual can be impressionable and self-sacrificing when it comes to dealing with children and romantic partners.

Neptune is the ruler of this empty house. If found in the twelfth, the nature is dreamy, impressionable and prone to escapism. Mediumistic tendencies are likely as intuition is acute and imagination is sharp. Creative skills are strong and success can be achieved through work related to art, poetry or music. The best work is done behind the scenes or in privacy, as periods of solitude and seclusion are often sought due to a highly sensitive nature. When it comes to relationships, there can be an attraction to secret romantic affairs. This would be a good placing for working in hospitals, the field of psychology or with disabled children.

If Neptune also forms a square with the Moon, the native can be indecisive, mentally confused or high strung. A clash between the subconscious and the conscious self may exist. Repressed emotions and nervousness can hinder common sense and intuitive faculties. It would be best to not place too much trust in romantic partners and to avoid all dubious, suspicious, or questionable alliances and schemes. Children, the mother or females in general can be source of sorrow, loss or self-undoing as secrets, trouble or deception may arise through these associations. This placing increases the need for fantasy, escapism and dreaming.

Fifth House Rulers

Regardless of the sign or ruling planet, we will briefly go through the ruler of the empty fifth houses as it may be positioned throughout the remaining 11 houses. Always consider the aspects formed with this planet as it provides the necessary information as to determining whether these energies are beneficial or challenging.

The ruler of the empty fifth house found in the sixth shows the tendency to attract romantic partners that start out as co-workers or are met through others at the workplace. The native is suited to work that provides creative challenges or opportunities. A successful hobby may be turned into profitable work. Working with children, romantic partners or young people in general are likely. This placing can bring benefits through jobs involving sports, financial speculation, holidays/vacations and the entertainment field or industry.

The ruler of the empty fifth house found in the seventh indicates a tendency toward always being involved in a major romantic relationship. The spouse is likely of a difference in age. Creative expression can be released through a marriage or partnership. Children are important within these long-term relationships. The need for fun and excitement within the marriage is strong.

The ruler of the empty fifth house found in the eighth shows that the individual is attracted to speculating with the finances of others. This would be a good placing for a banker, investor or stockbroker. Secrecy may surround the children or short-term romantic relations. Physical contact is important to the romantic life of this native.

The ruler of the empty fifth house found in the ninth indicates that many trips are likely taken with children or romantic partners. These romantic interests are often foreigners or encountered abroad. The self-expression is somewhat philosophical yet fun loving and optimistic. The mind is highly creative and explorative. This is a good placing for teaching, particularly young people and children. Hobbies may include foreign culture studies, philosophy or long distance travel.

The ruler of the empty fifth house found in the tenth increases the need for a career with plenty of opportunities for creative expression. A healthy ambition is likely. Careers involving sports, children and the entertainment field are likely to appeal. A hobby may be turned into a profitable a career. One in power of authority, such as a boss, may become a romantic partner.

The ruler of the empty fifth house found in the eleventh indicates that romantic partners often become friends and friends may become more than that. Younger friends are often chosen and children are also a source of friendship. Hopes and dreams can be achieved through creative expression or dealings with children.

The ruler of the empty fifth house found in the twelfth shows that the native is somewhat shy, introverted and secretive when it comes to the romantic life. The tendency toward secret romances is likely. Secrets may also involve children. Creativity is best expressed when in solitude, seclusion or behind the scenes. The native can be compassionate, self-sacrificing and highly intuitive with children and romantic partners.

The ruler of the empty fifth house found in the first brings a strong need for fun, entertainment and chance to explore creative potentials. This native projects the personality in a youthful and creative manner resulting in increased popularity. The tendency toward gambling or taking chances with romances is heightened.

The ruler of the empty fifth house found in the second reveals that a hobby may bring profits. This individual measures the self-worth against the potential for earning. Financial gains or losses may arise through romantic relationships, children, and creative efforts as well as through schemes involving sports and speculation.

The ruler of the empty fifth house found in the third indicates that manner of communication is likely youthful, fun, exciting, and highly creative and expressive. When it comes to romances, intellectual compatibility is important and required. Fun times can be spent with siblings and same age relatives. Creative writing can become a hobby.

The ruler of the empty fifth house found in the fourth brings much affection within the domestic circle. Children are important and always welcomed in the home. A creative hobby explored at home can be rewarding. This native is often involved in fun projects and activities with the family.

Empty Sixth House

The sixth house answers questions related to health, hygiene, diet, clothing, service, employment, co-workers and subordinates, as in people who work or would do work/jobs the native. It also represents the duties and services performed as well as describing the work environment. If the individual is unemployed, this house describes the people that are in contact with the native on a daily basis. The planetary ruler of this house when empty, is analyzed by the positions and aspects formed to other planets. The aspects describe the potential or challenges within this department of life.

Empty Sixth House Aries

This individual can be headstrong, assertive, competitive and impulsive at the work place or with co-workers and subordinates. Employment where there is little supervision and opportunities to initiate or implement new methods are sought. The native may be prone to headaches, fevers, burns and accidents, particularly at the work place.

Mars is the ruler of this empty house. If found in the second, potential for acquiring wealth and possessions through employment or health matters is increased. Reckless or impulsive spending should be avoided as financial losses may result that could affect the work or health. Health setbacks may also occur in the neck, ear or throat area as ruled by the second house.

If Mars also forms a conjunction with Pluto, the native possesses tremendous energy and will that is mainly expressed at the work place or with co-workers. The tendency to be aggressive, argumentative and domineering with co-workers or subordinates should be controlled. The temper is often tested through the work environment and matters related to finances. No one and nothing can stand in the way of this individual's financial or employment goals.

Empty Sixth House Taurus

This individual can be reliable and practical when it comes to work or health matters. Hard or physical labor tends to be avoided and work involving artistic or creative talents can bring success. The native cannot be rushed while working, as the tendency is to be patient and methodical. The throat, ear and neck area as ruled by this sign, can be prone to setbacks A taste for gourmet or rich foods may lead to being overweight. Exercise and moderation can prevent health problems. Change, particularly at the work place, is not handled easily as routine and monotony are preferred.

Venus is the ruler of this empty house. If positioned in the fifth, many romantic attachments can be formed through social activities, the work place or by being introduced to others through co-workers or subordinates. This placing emphasizes creative or artistic talent. The native is likely popular and well liked at work. Jobs involving children, teaching or financial speculation are often attracted. Hobbies, ruled by the fifth house, can lead to employment opportunities or financial rewards.

If Venus also forms a square with Neptune, the native is somewhat of an escapist in romance and jobs. Idealistic or unrealistic expectations can bring emotional upsets or problems. Dubious relationships, whether financial, working or romantic, should strongly be examined, as the tendency to be misled or victimized by these associations is likely. Overindulging in food, drink or drugs can negatively affect the health and job. A strong imagination can be put to good use in creative or artistic employment.

Empty Sixth House Gemini

This individual enjoys socializing at work where communication can be exchanged with others on a daily basis. However, too much talking or gossiping on the job can bring negative consequences. Employment providing change, variety and versatility is often sought as routine and monotony is avoided. Work must also offer a sense of independence, freedom and fun. More than one job at a time can easily be handled. Success can be found in sales, travel, teaching, lecturing or writing. In matters of health, extra care should be taken with the lungs, arms, shoulders and hands, particularly while working.

Mercury is the ruler of this empty house. If found in the twelfth, secrets are often kept or related at the work place. There is a marked interest in mysteries, psychology, dreams and occult topics. Many subconscious memories from past lives are likely as well as an active dream life. The native is likely shy, mysterious or withdrawn from others, especially while at work. Daily or work problems are best worked out alone in seclusion. This individual is suited to work involving secrecy, research, psychology or investigation or behind the scenes activity. Regular health check ups are recommended as hidden illnesses can develop.

If Mercury also forms a trine with Saturn, a good memory and reasoning abilities are likely. There is strong capacity for strenuous mental work as the mind is disciplined and good powers of concentration are likely. Profit, financial security and high status can be achieved through imaginative or intuitive talents. If the profession does not involve counseling or healing, chances are that this native is often found trying to solve the problems of fellow co-workers.

Empty Sixth House Cancer

This individual can be strongly influenced by emotions. Intuition is likely well developed as well as the capacity to sympathize with other's troubles. The tendency toward worrying should be controlled as moodiness or inconstant emotions can bring stomach setbacks. Many changes of employment are indicated as well as a need for work with constant change and activity. Profits can rise from creative ideas. There is a preference for working from the home. Regardless, the place of work must feel comfortable and secure. Keeping emotions in reign while at the workplace or when dealing with co-workers is recommended.

The Moon is the ruler of this empty house. If found in the fourth, a close and meaningful home life is strongly desired. Emotions are generally affected by family members or domestic issues. Being overly protective or worried about the health of a relative or parent is indicated. There is a strong indication of either working or living near water. Employment involving domestic products, land, farming, gardening, agriculture, real estate, nursing and the restaurant, hotel or service industry can be rewarding. This placing also strengthens the chances of success from working at home. Working with the parent represented by this house is evident as is the possibility of gaining employment through this parent.

If the Moon also forms an opposition with Uranus, emotional stress through work-related or family issues may affect the health, stomach or nervous system. Not only are many changes of employment indicated but that of residences as well. Changes of residence or jobs based upon impulse should strongly be avoided. Differences of opinion with a parent, particularly the mother, are indicated. An unstable or unusual childhood or relationship with a parent is likely.

Empty Sixth House Leo

This individual can be demanding of subordinates or co-workers. However, there is a strong need to gain their respect. Taking orders from others at the work place is not easily tolerated. Dramatic displays of behavior can be applied to get the most out of job situations, co-workers or subordinates. Work involving the entertainment industry or children can bring success. The health can be subject to setbacks of the heart, back and spine.

The Sun is the ruler of this empty house. If positioned in the second, the native can easily find material and financial success through work that is related to creative pursuits including art, film, drama, music and designing. Money is often spent on luxuries, possessions and items to proudly show off, particularly at the work place or to co-workers and subordinates. Emotional security is closely dependant upon financial security.

If the Sun also forms a trine with Neptune, intuition, imagination and creativity can be applied to increase wealth. Dealings or work related to liquids, gasses, water, the sea, photography and designing are likely attracted. This placing is also conducive to jobs involving healing or counseling, particularly to children as ruled by Leo.

Empty Sixth House Virgo

This native is prone to criticizing others, particularly co-workers and subordinates.

There is a tendency toward having high standards on the job as well as a need for a clean, orderly and organized working environment. Employment, where great attention to detail on a daily basis is required, can be successful. Professional success may also arise through work related to health and hygiene. Nervous or mental strain arising through over work or over worrying may affect the health.

Mercury is the ruler of this empty house. If found in the ninth, employment involving writing, communication, sales, education, travel, religion, spirituality, law and publishing are often of great interest. A literary, intellectual and highly communicative mind is likely. There is a great thirst for knowledge as well as the capacity for learning and dispensing this information to others. This would be an excellent placing for a teacher. Foreign languages or contacts are often related to employment matters.

If Mercury also forms a conjunction with the Moon, there is integration between the logical/reasoning intellect and the emotional/sub-conscious mind. Emotions are strong, imagination is rich and the memory is retentive and highly receptive. This individual seems to emotionally identify with females and excels in putting feelings into words.

Contacts with or connections through foreign females may further employment goals. The native will likely travel for work purposes or work in a foreign-based company. Working with females or foreigners is also indicated.

Empty Sixth House Libra

This individual can easily be influenced at the work place or by co-workers. The tendency to seek their approval and co-operation is indicated. Romantic relationships can easily be established at the work place or through co-workers. Pleasant relations with co-workers are essential to the native's well-being as well as harmonious working conditions and environment. Employment requiring social skills that involve public contact is likely of interest as well as jobs of a creative, artistic or legal nature. Hard work or physical labor however, tends to be shunned. Indecision and impressionability can hinder employment goals. Over indulgences should be avoided in order to prevent kidney disorders.

Venus is the ruler of this empty house. If found in the first, the tendency to be somewhat self-absorbed, particularly at the work place, is evident. Through employment is how the individuality and personality is best expressed. It is highly important to project a positive image at the work place, to co-workers and subordinates.

If Venus also forms a square with Mars, the tendency to become lazy, allowing others to do the native's work can mar progress. Feelings run deep and can easily be hurt due to a nature that is quickly offended. Emotional setbacks or conflicts are likely to arise through relationships established through the workplace. Secret romances formed through the job should be avoided. Extra tact should be used with male co-workers.

Empty Sixth House Scorpio

This individual is a determined, persevering and a resourceful employee. No task is too difficult to handle or tackle, as this native is a tireless worker with an abundance of energy and courage to draw upon when work becomes challenging. Jealousy, competition and secrecy often surround the working environment, however strong emotional ties can be developed with co-workers. To maintain harmonious working relations, the tendency to be domineering with co-workers and subordinates should be controlled. Employment related to research, investigation, forensic sciences, surgery, plumbing and law enforcement can be successful. The reproductive system may require frequent medical check-ups when Scorpio falls in this house of health.

Pluto is the ruler of this empty house. If positioned in the eleventh, friends can be influential at work or in achieving hopes and dreams as job contacts often include friends. Co-workers tend to become friends as powerful and often secretive ties are likely formed through the work place. Transformation and self-renewal can be achieved through work, friendships or group organizations. There is an element of intensity that exists within the pursuance of goals and wishes. This individual likely belongs to a group or club related to work. This is a good placing for work of a humanitarian nature such as a social worker as well as a group leader.

If Pluto also forms a sextile with Jupiter, business sense is likely highly developed. Teaching and law often attract. Many opportunities for employment are likely as Jupiter brings abundance and sextiles bring opportunities. The native can be most loyal to co-workers and friendships or group organizations. There is an ability or talent for bringing order out of chaos, particularly through work and among friendships.

Empty Sixth House Sagittarius

This native requires employment providing a certain amount of freedom and lack of routine. A job that involves travel and the outdoors can bring rewards as well as law, foreign business, higher learning, religion and spirituality. A sense of fun and adventure is often sought through the workplace and co-workers. When it comes to handing co-workers or subordinates, the speech can be blunt but honest. Over-indulging should strongly be avoided as the liver may suffer as a result.

Jupiter is the ruler of this empty house. If found in the eighth, chances are that the job involves the handling of other's finances such as wills, legacies taxes, banking and insurance matters. The choice of employment may also include matters related to sex, death, the occult or a job that is secretive somehow. A healthy and optimistic attitude regarding life, death and sex is evident.

If Jupiter also forms a square with Venus, the tendency to over-indulge is heightened. Carelessness at the workplace can produce costly errors as well as losing or wasting other people's money. Lawsuits related to employment or health matters may require special attention. Losses or lawsuits may also arise through gambling, romances, extravagances, love of luxury, a female, a co-worker or a subordinate. Romances, which are numerous, are often sought through the work place, as physical relationships with co-workers are likely.

Empty Sixth House Capricorn

This native tends to be reserved, private, ambitious, rational and practical in work matters. There is a strong ability to work hard. Patience, determination, self-control and good organizational skills are likely. Relationships with subordinates or co-workers may be somewhat distant or unemotional. This individual is not a fast worker who socializes on the job, but rather a dependable and persevering employee who gets things done.

Saturn is the ruler of this empty house. If found in the tenth, a self-reliant and ambitious nature is expressed while at work and throughout the career. There is a strong desire for stability and position of high status. Positions of authority and responsibility are well handled as work relations and career matters are taken most seriously. Professional success comes after the age of thirty. The parent ruled by this house may be instrumental in finding the native employment.

If Saturn also forms trine with Mars, career success, stability and high status are almost assured as promotions through hard work and efforts are likely. Executive ability and managerial skills are also present that can be used to further professional goals.

Empty Sixth House Aquarius

This individual requires employment that provides a certain amount of independence and spontaneity as well as requiring mental creativity and originality. Routine is not easily handled as unusual, unexpected and unorthodox methods or situations are preferred, particularly among co-workers, subordinates and within the work place. Co-workers often become friends and unusual ties result. Work involving computers, aviation, mathematics, electricity, engineering, television and radio, machines, psychology, the media, social work and astrology can also be rewarding choices for employment.

Uranus is the ruler of this empty house. If positioned in the third, a perceptive, inventive and mathematical mind is indicated. This native is not easily influenced or persuaded. The intellect is quick, intuitive, inventive and fascinated by the unconventional. There can be something unusual or original about the manner of speech or communication. Sudden and short trips related to work are likely to be taken. Flashes of inspiration and unusual ideas can be explored through the employment.

If Uranus also forms a square with Mars, accidents, peculiar incidents or unexpected disruptions are likely to occur while commuting, traveling short distances or at the work place. Working with machinery can be dangerous. Separation or arguments involving siblings, same age relatives, neighbors, subordinates or co-workers often take place due to the native's temper and lack of patience. Jumping to conclusions and impulsive actions while at work or during short distance travels should strongly be reconsidered. Danger of accidents to the ankle area are likely.

Empty Sixth House Pisces

This individual is secretive, shy and can be a most devoted employee. Feelings can be most sensitive and easily hurt particularly with co-workers and while at work. There is great sensitivity to subordinates and co-workers, therefore, being deceived or easily influenced by these people should strongly be avoided. Intuition can be successfully applied to work and health matters, however, there is danger of becoming lazy, lacking in concentration or being indecisive while at work. Daydreaming on the job may relieve stress but produce errors. On account of a sympathetic and compassionate nature, the native is often sought out for advice or counsel by co-workers. This is a good placing for employment as a counselor, advisor or therapist. Other areas include jobs related to the sea, liquids, music, dance, photography, art, chemistry, healing and spirituality. Excessive worrying over work and health matters should be controlled. Overindulging is to be avoided and extra caution is required when using medication in order to avoid infections or poisons. The emotions can play a dominant role in health matters and psychosomatic illnesses are also likely. A close connection and deep understanding with animals or pets is evident.

Neptune is the ruler of this empty house. If found in the seventh, the spouse may be introduced through the job or a co-worker. The marriage partner may be a co-worker as well or tends to be compassionate and artistic. Partnerships, whether marriage or business, are likely formed with co-workers or subordinates where a psychic bond often exists. Conditions of the work place can affect these relationships and these partnerships in turn, can affect the job.

If Neptune also forms a trine with the Sun, marriage, partnerships and working relationships are of great significance. Intuition is exchanged and creative expressions are shared with the spouse, co-worker or partner. Working together on artistic projects or work can bring success, as each is able to inspire and draw out the other's creative potential.

Sixth House Rulers

Regardless of the sign or ruling planet, we will briefly go through the ruler of the empty sixth house as it may be positioned throughout the remaining 11 houses. Always consider the aspects formed with this planet as it provides the necessary information as to determining whether these energies are beneficial or challenging.

The ruler of the empty sixth house found in the seventh reveals an individual who may marry or form a partnership with a co-worker, or the spouse or partner may be met through work-related ties. There can be much competition or rivalry with others at work. The job may affect or influence the marriage or partnership.

The ruler of the empty sixth house found in the eighth indicates that the native may be employed in matters related to handling other's finances, such as a banker or investor. Work involving matters of the dead, such as insurance, taxes and wills may also attract. Other job possibilities include surgery, the occult and work related to sex. Secretive, physical relationships may develop with co-workers or through job-related conditions.

The ruler of the empty sixth house found in the ninth reveals a personality that requires intellectual freedom or opportunities for exploration, particularly at the work place. The mentality is communicating, inspiring, expansive and optimistic. This is a good placing for teaching, law, foreign culture or business, religion, lecturing, advertising, writing, publishing, education, television, radio and travel as a profession. The choice of employment may also take this individual to another country or involve foreign co-workers or subordinates.

The ruler of the empty sixth house found in the tenth brings a tendency to being ambitious at the work place. Leadership qualities are evident and positions of authority are handled with ease. A strong need for respect from co-workers and subordinates is evident. Promotions are frequent and can lead to high social or professional status. The reputation is mainly based upon the native's work as a self-reliant, motivated and efficient employee.

The ruler of the empty sixth house found in the eleventh increases the chances of gaining employment through friends and group associations. Friendships are often formed with co-workers or through the work place. This is a good placing for employment related to social and humanitarian causes. Unexpected situations often arise through the work and unusual ties can be formed with co-workers or subordinates. The choice of work must provide freedom, independence and unexpected, exciting or unusual opportunities.

The ruler of the empty sixth house found in the twelfth reveals the tendency to obtain work that is quiet, peaceful, behind the scenes and performed in seclusion. Daily moments of solitude bring peace of mind and calm the nerves. The element of escapism or secrecy often surrounds the working environment or the relationships formed within. This is a good placing for a work involving medicine, psychology, healing and places of confinement, such as hospitals or prisons. Hidden illnesses that are difficult to diagnose may arise if precautions are not taken.

The ruler of the empty sixth house found in the first indicates that the native tends to easily project the personality and self-expression through work. Personal health matters and hygiene may be of particular interest. It is important for this native to appear healthy, clean and well employed.

The ruler of the empty sixth house found in the second shows that the individual's motivation for work is purely financial and monetary gains through employment are likely achieved. Work provides a strong sense of material security and self-worth as emotional and financial security largely depends upon employment. Financial goals can be realized through hard work, rather than through chance, luck or other people.

The ruler of the empty sixth house found in the third brings a tendency to be employed in fields involving communication, transport, education and writing. Frequent short distance travels may be taken related to the job and commuting to work is also likely. Work can involve or be obtained through a sibling, neighbor or same generation relative. The job itself must be intellectually stimulating.

The ruler of the empty sixth house found in the fourth indicates the possibility of working with family or a parent. Employment may also be gained through the parent ruled by this house. Working from the home is evident and other job possibilities include such fields as real estate, domestic and healing products or services, the food or hotel industry, agriculture, building, architecture and the antique and furniture business.

The ruler of the empty sixth house found in the fifth indicates that romantic partners are often encountered through work or introduced by co-workers or subordinates. A job requiring the expression of creative talent on a daily basis is often attracted and likely successful. This placing also indicates talent for working with children, such as healing, counseling or teaching.

Empty Seventh House

The seventh house answers questions involving partnerships whether business, marriage or long-term and live-in relationships. As the fifth house rules romance and dating, the seventh represents relationships where a commitment has been made between the two people.

The first house, or Ascendant, represents the native's individuality, the opposite seventh house, or Descendant represents the marriage partner that is likely attracted as well as conditions within the relationship. The seventh house also rules people whom we seek counsel, such as advisors and lawyers as well as open enemies, rivals and competitors. We also look to this house when seeking answers to lawsuits or legal contracts and matters. The planetary ruler of this house when empty, is analyzed by the position and aspects formed to other planets. The aspects describe the potential or challenges within this department of life.

Empty Seventh House Aries

This individual tends to become involved with emotionally impulsive, aggressive, energetic and impatient partners. Important relationships are likely formed with those that have the Sun, Moon or Ascendant in Aries or Libra. Marriage may be early in life and begin rather suddenly. The spirit of competition is well developed as well as the capability of motivating or leading others. Although the Ascendant is Libra, the sign of partnerships, there is a strong desire for independence within these relationships as well as the need to prove the self-worth within the marriage or partnership.

Mars is the ruler of this empty house. If found in the ninth, the native is highly enthusiastic about travel, learning, exploring and adventure, particularly with a partner or spouse. The partner selected may be encountered abroad, through legal matters or while pursuing a higher education. The spouse or partner is likely of a foreign background or nationality.

If Mars also forms an opposition with Uranus, sudden or unexpected trouble while traveling, with legal matters or with in-laws can be expected. Controlling outbursts of temper can help maintain amicable relationships with the spouse, in-laws and foreigners. The opposition from Uranus in the third house suggests applying tact and consideration with siblings, same age relatives and neighbors as well. The choice of partner or spouse is also likely to have Aquarius prominent.

Empty Seventh House Taurus

This native strongly requires stability and financial security within the marriage or partnership. Financial partnerships can bring success with reliable and trustworthy individuals. The type of spouse or business partner attracted has a Taurus or Scorpio Sun, Moon or Ascendant. Loyalty and dependability are well developed within these relationships.

Venus is the ruler of this empty house. If found in the eleventh, many female friends and companions are likely. A spouse or business partner may become a friend or a friend may develop into a spouse or partner. The choice of marriage or business partner may also be introduced by friends or encountered through group or club associations. Romantic and financial opportunities often arise through friendships or group organizations.

If Venus also forms a square with the Moon, the spouse, partner, mother, a friend or group organization can bring financial or emotional setbacks. The mother or a female friend may interfere within the marriage or business partnership. Emotional outbursts are common with the marriage or partnership. Precautions should be taken when entering into joint financial or legal agreements with a friend, spouse or partner. The choice of partner or spouse is also likely to have Cancer prominent.

Empty Seventh House Gemini

This native prefers intellectual relationships where ideas can be exchanged with a partner or spouse. The individual prefers the company of others as interaction and communication are sought. A sociable and communicative nature is evident as well as the ability to adapt to changing circumstances within a long-term relationship. The partner selected is often younger in age, versatile, lively, witty, intelligent and young at heart. A marriage or partnership formed with one born under a Gemini or Sagittarius Sun, Moon or Ascendant is likely. This placing tends to indicate more than one marriage.

Mercury is the ruler of this empty house. If positioned in the second, this native is able to financially gain or lose through the marriage or business partnership if care is not taken.

Verbal skills and valuable ideas may increase wealth. There is much communication involving money within the marriage or partnership. A marriage or partnership for money is not ruled out. Work requiring communication, public speaking, negotiations or sales can bring financial security.

If Mercury also forms a trine with Jupiter, financial gains from intellectual efforts and big ideas are almost assured. Wealth can be achieved through a spouse or partner as well. There is an interest in foreign lands or cultures where the spouse or business partner can be encountered. A happy marriage or partnership is likely with this placing. A flair for business is likely as well as the chances for gaining financially through such ventures involving communication, writing, law, finances, counseling young people, publishing, sales, travel and teaching.

Empty Seventh House Cancer

This individual is attracted to sensitive relationships and partnerships where emotional and domestic security is sought. The personality is receptive and devoted toward those involved in these unions. The tendency to choose a spouse or partner with maternal and protective traits is evident. The choice of partner or spouse often has a Cancer or Capricorn Sun, Moon or Ascendant.

The Moon is the ruler of this empty house. If found in the first, the native generally prefers being alone than in the company of others. A strong imagination is evident as well as a desire for frequent change and travel due to a restless nature. Moods, feelings and emotions play an important role in the native's decision-making abilities. Imagination and intuition is strong particularly when it comes to understanding the spouse or partner. This position indicates the possibility of seeing the self through the eyes of others and being able to easily sympathize with the problems of others, particularly the spouse or partner.

If the Moon also forms a square with Saturn, the personality is likely most sensitive, shy, inconsistent and not easily revealed to others. The relationship with a parent may be lacking in warmth due to early childhood issues. Letting go of the past is highly recommended. This aspect often indicates shyness and inhibitions with the spouse or partner due to a lack of self-esteem. The tendency to select an older spouse or partner is indicated. There is danger of feelings of depression, loneliness and pessimism that should strongly be controlled. Facing life with renewed vitality and optimism is the key to working with this aspect. The choice of spouse or partner may also be born with Capricorn prominent.

Empty Seventh House Leo

This individual is romantic, playful and dramatic when it comes to important relationships. The marriage or business partner is highly influential, generous, loyal and confident. The spouse or partner selected is likely born under a Sun, Moon or Ascendant in

Leo or Aquarius. The marriage or business partner must be committed and devoted to the relationship.

The Sun is the ruler of this empty house. If positioned in the fourth, the native can benefit from real estate dealings, particularly with the spouse, business partner or the parent represented by this house. Children and family ties are important within the marriage or partnership. As this house rules the second half of life, marital success is more likely to occur then. Clinging to past important long term relationships can bring emotional setbacks.

If the Sun also forms a trine with Pluto, a marriage or partnership can beneficially transform the native. The capacity to lead or inspire others is likely well developed due to a strong personality and well-developed self-confidence. Domestic felicity is emphasized. The native may possess a gift for solving other's problems. The choice of spouse or partner may also have Scorpio prominent.

Empty Seventh House Virgo

This native is somewhat shy, cautious, critical, reserved and inhibited when in comes to important relationships such as marriage or partnerships. Problems or situations in this area are approached with common sense and very carefully thought out. There must be intellectual compatibility with the spouse or partner for the relationship to progress. The tendency to be highly selective and logical when it comes to choosing a partner is evident due to a tendency to be discriminative with high expectations. Marriage is likely to take place with one who has the Sun, Moon or Ascendant in Virgo or Pisces. This individual is attracted to a spouse or partner that is hardworking, intelligent, practical, efficient and reserved.

Mercury is the ruler of this empty house. If found in the sixth, marriage or a business partnership can be formed with a co-worker, subordinate or employee. The tendency to over-work is evident as Virgo by nature, is a hard working sign. The mind is logical, receptive and analytical, particularly when it comes to marriage, partnerships and employment. As this is the house of health, nervous tension and over-worry can bring setbacks. The choice of employment likely involves work that requires a sharp intellect or strong imagination.

If Mercury also forms a conjunction with Venus, the ability to charm, organize and negotiate within the marriage or partnership is evident. The manner of communicating is likely charming and eloquent. There is a strong dislike of partners of any kind that are rough, rude, crude or loud. The job may lead to romance, marriage or a partnership. An important relationship in turn, may also lead to employment. The choice of marriage or business partner is also likely to have Taurus or Libra prominent.

Empty Seventh House Libra

This individual is constantly involved in a special relationship where upon much importance is placed. However, indecisiveness when it comes to choosing partners is also evident. There is an attraction to spouse or partners that are refined, graceful, social, and intellectual. Although Aries rises on the Ascendant, there is great sensitivity to others. There is the tendency to project the personality through relationships and to seek their approval. Marriage or partnerships formed with one who has the Sun, Moon or Ascendant in Aries or Libra works out the best.

Venus is the ruler of this empty house. If found in the eighth, financial gains through partnerships or marriage are indicated. These unions may also be formed on the basis of possible financial advancement. Physical relationships are often intense. Secrets may plague a marriage or partnership. An inheritance from a spouse or partner is likely.

If Venus also forms a square with Neptune, losses through spouse or partner may arise due to imaginary problems, delusion, deception, lack of honesty, alcohol or drug abuse.

The spouse or partner may be extravagant and somewhat of a dreamer. Relationships may be used as means of escape. Unreliable partners are often chosen resulting in emotional disappointments. Legal problems may often hit snags or not work out as hoped. The tendency to be mislead, misunderstood, victimized, fooled or easily persuaded by others is to be strongly controlled. The choice of spouse or partner may also have Pisces prominent.

Empty Seventh House Scorpio

This native is emotionally intense and sensitive when it comes to handling marriage or partnerships. Secret alliances are likely formed with others. It would be best to control feelings of suspicion, betrayal or jealousy as relationships may suffer. Physical desires are strong within the marriage or partnership. As this is the sign of transformation, a sense of rebirth and renewal arises within the marriage or partnership. Long-term compatibility is found with one born with the Sun, Moon or Ascendant in Taurus or Scorpio. There is a strong attraction to spouses or partners that are strong-willed, magnetic, secretive and passionate. As a competitor, there is an element of ruthlessness and desire to win at all costs. This individual possesses a profound ability to see through others and their motives.

Pluto is the ruler of this empty house. If found in the twelfth, gains are likely acquired through involvements that are hidden, secret or behind the scenes. A spouse or partner may be hospitalized for long term or may be met through establishments of confinement. Secret affairs are emphasized with this placing, however it would not be easy for a spouse or partner to keep secrets from the native. A marriage or partnership can be spiritually rejuvenating or enlightening. This is an excellent position for a psychologist or marriage counselor as well as for matters requiring research and investigation.

If Pluto also forms a trine with the Moon, emotions are intense but can be properly channeled and maintained under control. Powers of persuasion, courage and determination are well developed. Business ability and creative talent is evident. This aspect is also conducive to work involving counseling, social welfare, financial advice, physical healing, therapy and public relations. The choice of spouse or partner may also have Cancer prominent.

Empty Seventh House Sagittarius

This individual is friendly, open, outgoing and often attracted to foreign spouses or partners. Two marriages are likely and compatibility can be found with one who has the Sun, Moon or Ascendant in Gemini or Sagittarius. Potential partners for marriage or business relationships are often found among the equally outgoing, optimistic, humorous, and adventurous. There is a strong need for exploration and freedom with the marriage or partnership in order to prevent boredom and restlessness from setting in.

Jupiter is the ruler of this empty house. If positioned in the fifth, the social life is highly active and quite busy. Financial luck and opportunities can be expected or losses experienced due to over-optimism and extravagance. Sports events and any form of recreation are often enjoyed with the spouse or partner. Children are many and can be a major source of joy to the marriage or partnership.

If Jupiter also forms a square with the Sun, the native may suffer financial losses through the marriage, the partnership, children or foreign and legal matters. These setbacks may also stem from self-indulgences, dishonest behavior and gambling. Often, more is taken on than can be handled and therefore many promises are left unfulfilled. The choice of spouse or partner may also have Leo prominent.

Empty Seventh House Capricorn

This individual possesses a serious, reserved and conservative outlook on marriage and partnerships. The choice of spouse or partner is either older or has the Sun, Moon or Ascendant in Cancer or Capricorn. Marriage and partnerships are likely delayed or formed later in life and are often a great source of responsibility with this placing. The relationship can be lacking in emotion or affection but has the tendency to be long-lasting. There is an attraction to partners that are dependable, stable and career-oriented or hard working.

Saturn is the ruler of this empty house. If found in the twelfth, the native may find a spouse or partner while involved in behind the scenes activities or in places of confinement. There is a great need for solitude, particularly within marriage or partnerships. The chances of entering into secret partnerships are strong. Little is revealed to others due to a lack of confidence, however fears and limitations are likely self-imposed, particularly those involving marriage or partnerships. As this the house of karma, it is likely that there is unfinished business from a former life that needs to be handled with a spouse or partner in this life. Competitors and open enemies may evolve into secret enemies.

If Saturn also forms an opposition with the Sun, many doubts and responsibilities are likely to involve the marriage and partnership. There is a feeling of being tied down in this area. Trouble or secret sorrows may arise from within the marriage or business partnership as well from enemies, adversaries or legal matters. The partner may be somewhat cold and critical or have Leo prominent. This position brings the possibility of becoming a recluse at some point.

Empty Seventh House Aquarius

This native is emotionally independent within the marriage or partnership as the need for freedom here is strong. Unconventional or unusual relationships tend to be formed with those that are friendly, unusual, unpredictable, exciting and independent. A friend may become a spouse or partner. Platonic relationships are easily maintained and the choice of marriage or business partner must also be a friend. The partner selected will have the Sun, Moon or Ascendant in Leo or Aquarius. Sudden disruptions, surprises or separations can be frequent within these relationships.

Uranus is the ruler of this empty house. If found in the tenth, the career can be linked to the marriage or business partnership. An employer, boss or superior can become a spouse or partner. The marriage partner may also be met through the career. Unusual or unexpected conditions may also surround the career or reputation.

If Uranus also forms a trine with Mercury, good communication within the career and marriage is indicated. Intuition is enhanced and can be used to gain marital or professional success. This is an excellent placing for a counseling astrologer, salesperson, writer, teacher or public speaker. The choice of marriage or business partner may also have Gemini or Virgo prominent.

Empty Seventh House Pisces

This individual can be over-sensitive when it comes to handling issues within the marriage or partnership. The element of secrecy, self-sacrifice or escapism within the relationship is evident. Two marriages or partnerships are likely when this dual sign rules the marriage house. There is an attraction to sympathetic, romantic, devoted and spiritual partners. The spouse or partner selected will have the Sun, Moon or Ascendant in Virgo or Pisces. This placing indicates that a psychic connection exists with the marriage or business partnership.

Neptune is the ruler of this empty house. If found in the third, communication becomes highly important within the marriage or partnership. A strong imagination and psychic link within the relationship is emphasized. The spouse or business partner can be met while commuting or traveling short distances or can be introduced through a sibling or same generation relative. Literary talent is indicated particularly in the fiction or romance genre.

If Neptune also forms a square with Mercury, there native would do best to implement honesty whenever possible. It is important to be particularly clear when communicating to others, especially the spouse, partner or siblings. Extra caution should be applied to prevent being swindled or victimized within these relationships. Care should always be taken when forming partnerships, agreements or signing documents. Intuitive powers can be unreliable. The choice of marriage or business partner may also have Gemini or Virgo prominent.

Seventh House Ruler

Regardless of the sign or ruling planet, we will briefly go through the ruler of the empty seventh house as it may be positioned throughout the remaining 11 houses. Always consider the aspects formed with this planet as it provides the necessary information as to determining whether these energies are beneficial or challenging.

The ruler of the empty seventh house found in the eighth indicates that finances will be affected by the marriage or partnership. The death of the spouse or partner can bring financial gains or losses. There can be an element of secrecy involving these relationships. Finances may be the motive for marriage or forming a partnership. Sex is very important within the marriage.

The ruler of the empty seventh house found in the ninth increases the chances of marrying a foreigner or encountering this person or partner while in a land faraway or in an institution of higher education. This is a good placing for a lawyer. Legal matters are likely to involve a partnership or marriage.

The ruler of the empty seventh house found in the tenth indicates that a marriage or partnership is likely formed with an older, more established individual or a boss or superior. The spouse or partner can be encountered through the career or is instrumental in furthering the native's career goals. The parent ruled by this house may also introduce the marriage or business partner to the native. Long-term relationships can be initiated in order to enhance the career or status and reputation.

The ruler of the empty seventh house found in the eleventh reveals that a friend could become a spouse or partner. This partner in turn, must also be a friend. Hopes and dreams can be realized through the marriage or a partnership. The spouse or business partner can be introduced through a friendship or group organization.

The ruler of the empty seventh house found in the twelfth indicates that many secrets exist within the marriage or partnership. There is much compassion and need for solitude or privacy within these relationships. The marriage or partnership may be a karmic relationship that requires lessons to be learned in the present life. The spouse or partner may be met through places of confinement or behind the scenes activities. There can be a fear of long-term commitments with others. Public enemies, as ruled by the seventh house such as competitors or rivals, can also become secret enemies, as ruled by the twelfth house. This is a good placing for a marriage or psychological counselor.

The ruler of the empty seventh house found in the first increases the need for a marriage or partnership, as this is how the native's personality is measured and best projected. It is important for this individual to express the self-image through long-term relationships. However, being influenced by others should strongly be avoided. The spouse or partner selected can be mirror image of this individual.

The ruler of the empty seventh house found in the second reveals the importance of financial and material security within a marriage or partnership. This native may marry or form a partnership based on the possibility of financial gain and material security.

The ruler of the empty seventh house found in the third brings a strong need for communication and intellectual compatibility within the marriage or partnership. The spouse or partner can be met through short distance travel or while commuting as well as through a sibling, neighbor or and same generation relative. A sibling, neighbor or same generation relative may become a marriage or business partner.

The ruler of the empty seventh house found in the fourth indicates that the home life and domestic environment is of utmost importance within the marriage or partnership. The spouse may be introduced through the family or parent ruled by this house. Business dealings with a spouse or partner are likely to involve domestic products, land, property or real estate.

The ruler of the empty seventh house found in the fifth increases the chances of having many romantic partners and long-term relationships. Children are important within these special relationships. The element of fun is important to the marriage or partnership and should provide an outlet for creativity and amusement. A younger spouse or business partner is likely.

The ruler of the empty seventh house found in the sixth reveals that the spouse or partner can be met the work place as a subordinate or co-worker may become a marriage or business partner. The health of a spouse or partner may require attention. This placing can indicate that the individual is married to the job

Empty Eighth House

The eighth house answers questions involving other people's finances, inheritances, legacies, joint resources, loans, taxes, wills, investments and insurance matters. It also represents birth, death, sex, secrets, spirituality, the afterlife and matters of the occult. The planetary ruler of this house when empty, is analyzed by the position and aspects formed to other planets. The aspects describe the potential or challenges within this department of life.

Empty Eighth House Aries

This individual tends to be impulsive when it comes to matters involving the finances of others. There is the ability to form quick ideas and methods for improving or acquiring finances, however impatience and hasty decisions can sabotage profitable returns. As Aries is a competitive and aggressive sign, this would be a good placing for business ventures. Strong physical desires are evident. This placing often brings little fear of death.

Mars is the ruler of this empty house. If found in the tenth, there is attraction to careers involving death, psychiatry, surgery, sexuality, the occult, research, investigation and the management of other's finances. This is also a good position for a financial advisor or investor. The tendency to compete with others in order to achieve a prominent status is likely. An assertive or aggressive reputation within the career is evident. Promotion or career advancement may come as a result of another's demise. Some sort of secret or mystery may involve the profession.

If Mars also forms a square with the Sun, secret relationships with bosses or superiors are likely. The possibility to use sex in order to advance professionally is not ruled out. Conflicts over other's finances may arise, particularly with males. A partnership or the spouse can be a source of financial setbacks. Accidents, particularly at the workplace due to recklessness or impulsiveness, should always be avoided. It is important to cultivate patience and self-control, particularly within the career and to stay clear of risky financial or career moves.

Empty Eighth House Taurus

Taurus is the sign representing money and in this house indicates the tendency to earn through marriage or partnerships. The ability to increase finances through land, property, real estate and secretive or mysterious sources is also evident. Sensuality and physical pleasures are enhanced, however self-indulgences are to be avoided in the romantic area. This individual is persistent and reliable when it comes to handling the finances of others.

Venus is the ruler of this empty house. If positioned in the fourth, family inheritances are likely, particularly from the parent ruled by this house. The tendency toward being highly protective of family and material possessions is evident. There can be secrets involving the childhood, the home life, a parent or a family member. Not only is the native able to acquire financial gains through land or real estate dealings, but through domestic products or services, the hotel industry, agriculture and farming.

If Venus also forms a trine with Jupiter, secure and safe financial or family investments can bring considerable profit. This placing brings luck and success in business matters. Earning ability is well developed and can result in the accumulation of wealth and possessions through others. Joyful family relations are likely.

Empty Eighth House Gemini

This individual tends to verbally express physical desires, emotions and secrets. Topics of frequent conversation include financial matters, sexuality, death, the afterlife and the occult, as there is great curiosity about these subjects. Chances are this native enjoys a good mystery and may possess talent in writing this genre for profit.

Mercury is the ruler of this empty house. If found in the first, an ability to acquire finances and material possessions through personal efforts are evident. There is a deep need to get to the bottom of things, particularly if the native is somehow involved. It is difficult for this individual to keep secrets. Gains through communication, writing, the intellect or the literary field are likely.

If Mercury also forms an opposition with Mars, an argumentative nature, a short temper and a sharp tongue tends to arouse animosity in others. Impulsiveness and jumping to conclusions can bring financial losses. The native strongly dislikes being criticized as it is interpreted as a personal attack. Heated topics of arguments or debate include death, sexuality, the occult, joint resources and the finances of others. Spoken words often end up being regretted.

Empty Eighth House Cancer

When it comes to joint resources or other's finances, there is much intuition and receptivity resulting in good business sense. Talent for research is pronounced and memory is enhanced with this position. Finances of the spouse or partner can be fluctuating. There is an intensity of feeling as this is a water sign in a water house. Emotional security is sought through the expression of physical romantic activity. A family separation or death marks a turning point in life. Inheritance from the mother or a female is likely. Secrets often involve the domestic life, the mother or a member of the maternal side of the family. Much caution is to be used when near or in water.

The Moon is the ruler of this empty house. If positioned in the ninth, financial benefits are likely to arise through foreigners, females, travel, publishing, domestic products, hotel or restaurant industry, institutions of learning and businesses in general. Long trips are often taken as travel brings emotional security. A home by water may also be established far from the place of birth or childhood.

If the Moon also forms a conjunction with Jupiter, this native can reap rewards through travel, foreign contacts, higher education, teaching, law, religion, publishing or while in a far off country. A fertile imagination and big ideas can bring financial profit. There is a tendency to be most generous with the finances of others. This placing benefits spiritual research and the mastering of different languages.

Empty Eighth House Leo

This individual can be competitive and generous with joint resources or the finances of others. The native possesses a healthy outlook on sexuality, death and the mysteries of life. There is strong faith in the unknown and the higher powers. Exerting the heart or back can bring serious consequences in later years.

The Sun is the ruler of this empty house. If found in the second, material wealth and possessions can easily be acquired as earning abilities show promise. Financial gains through influential people or connections are evident. Wealth may come through a death, legacy, will, deed or insurance matters. Emotional and financial security largely depends upon each other.

If the Sun also forms a trine with Neptune, intuition and imagination are tools available for increasing wealth. Creative and inspired ideas can produce financial successes. Business dealings with gasses, liquids, water, the sea, photography, film, art, dance and music can be rewarding.

Empty Eighth House Virgo

This native can be somewhat inhibited or discreet when it comes to physical romantic relationships. Matters related to other people's finances are handled in a rational, frugal, down to earth and analytical manner. Finances can be improved through practical ideas and services performed for others. This individual is suited to professions involving taxes, health, death, corporate finances and insurance. The intellect is probing, dissecting, clear and logical as the ability to get to the bottom and root of things is pronounced. There is skepticism regarding occult subjects and mysteries of life.

Mercury is the ruler of this empty house. If found in the sixth, the native may choose a profession involving the management or handling of other's finances. Teaching, public speaking, writing and communication in general can be rewarding jobs as well as work requiring research and detailed analysis. Regardless, the job must provide intellectual challenges or stimulation. There is a tendency to excessive worry about matters related to death, taxes, insurance, work, sexuality or health.

If Mercury also forms a square with Pluto, preoccupation or obsession with trivial details may hinder intellectual progress. The nature can be suspicious, nervous and secretive. The manner of speech can be blunt and to the point, regardless of how it may affect others. Heated arguments over joint resources or power struggles with co-workers are evident.

Empty Eighth House Libra

This individual possesses a balanced and impartial outlook regarding, sexuality, the occult, death and taxes. Hesitation due to indecision may hinder financial progress. The marriage or partnership can strengthen financial resources or may be based upon the hope of acquiring wealth. Inheritance from a spouse, partner or social contact is also evident.

Venus is the ruler of this empty house. If found in the fifth, inheritance may also come from children or romantic partners. Financial gains are likely achieved through matters related to sports, speculation, stocks, theatre, entertainment, games, creativity, hobbies or children. This is a good placing for a child psychologist or counselor. Romantic relationships tend to be highly physical as the nature is most passionate.

If Venus also forms a conjunction with the Moon, the individual has many female friends. A family inheritance, particularly from the mother or her side of the family, is evident. Finances can also be improved through matters related to domestic products and services as well as the hotel or restaurant industry. Indecision, overindulgence or a love of luxury may hinder financial goals. Emotions are intensified and the tendency toward possessiveness should be controlled.

Empty Eighth House Scorpio

This individual can be highly emotional and intense. Strong physical romantic desires are present as the nature is most passionate. Secrets often involve sexuality, death, the occult, joint resources or the finances acquired through others. The native is resourceful, intuitive, courageous and private. There is talent in matters requiring research and investigation.

Pluto is the ruler of this empty house. If positioned in the third, a deep, curious and penetrating mind is evident. No mystery is too difficult for this native to unravel. Strong opinions are often expressed but much is kept within. Concentration skills and memory are well above average. Finances can be acquired through communication or literary interests. An inheritance may come from a sibling, same generation relative or neighbor.

If Pluto also forms a trine with Mars, the native is emotionally, mentally and physically balanced. Ambition, determination, will power and physical strength are pronounced. Confidence, constructive energy and courage are also available when needed. This placing often indicates a lack of fear and intimidation from others.

Empty Eighth House Sagittarius

This individual can be sexually open and honest with the spouse or partner. There is great fascination or curiosity with foreign lands or cultures, spiritual matters, the occult, religion or the afterlife. An explorative, optimistic or extravagant nature when it comes to matters involving death, the occult, sexuality and finances acquired through others is evident.

Jupiter is the ruler of this empty house. If found in the seventh, the native can financially benefit through marriage or partnerships. There is a strong sense of morality combined with sexuality in these relationships. However, the marriage or partnership may also be formed on the basis of possible financial gain. An inheritance from the spouse or partner is likely. Secrets involving joint finances are evident.

If Jupiter also forms an opposition with Mercury, the native is likely to experience financial losses through marriage, partnerships, insurance, taxes or death. Over-generosity, promising more than can be delivered and extra marital activities can also bring monetary setbacks. Much caution is required when handling lawsuits and legal matters, as it is very important for this individual to carefully read the fine print before entering or signing agreements. The tendency to exaggerate, procrastinate and be skeptical of others is to be avoided.

Empty Eighth House Capricorn

This individual can be emotionally reserved and may have difficulty in expressing feelings within the marriage or partnership. The native is likely sexually inhibited, conservative or most cautious, as there is much self-control in this area. A rational, responsible and down to earth approach is taken when dealing with matters related to death, taxes, legacies, joint resources, insurance and the finances acquired through others. A long life is often indicated with this placing.

Saturn is the ruler of this empty house. If found in the eleventh, the native's friends may be among the older, career-oriented or professional type. Friendships may be karmic and few in number but can be enduring. These associations can bring either a sense of stability and responsibility or burdens and hardships. There can be a somewhat detached or cold attitude toward friendships or group associations. The native may be demanding and expect too much from friends. Patience, persistence, determination and hard work can make dreams and wishes come true.

If Saturn also forms a square with the Sun, caution should always be applied with dealing with older and influential friends as they can bring financial setbacks. Male friends in particular, may impede the native's dreams from coming true. Self-expression is hindered or blocked from friendships due to a lack of self-confidence.

Empty Eighth House Aquarius

This native requires emotional independence and freedom within the marriage or partnership. Unusual or unexpected circumstances may surround such matters as death, insurance, taxes, legacies and earnings acquired through others, marriage or partnerships. Originality, unpredictability and innovative ideas regarding the handling or acquisition of other's finances are also evident. There is an open, curious and inquisitive outlook regarding the mysteries of life and occult subjects. Physically romantic relationships can be unconventional, ending as abruptly as they began or tend to involve friends or unusual people. The loss of friendships can deeply be felt.

Uranus is the ruler of this empty house. If found in the twelfth, there is talent for matters requiring research, investigation, intuition and counseling. The native is secretive and tends to keep in the background engaged in behind the scenes activities. Organizations of a secretive nature can be most appealing. A spiritual attraction to the unusual, unconventional or the occult is evident. Frequent periods of seclusion pondering the mysteries of life can bring personal transformation. Shady financial dealings can bring hospitalization or imprisonment.

If Uranus also forms a sextile with Venus, finances can be improved through females, partnerships or marriage. Perception is acute and mind is alert and inspiring. Artistic talent and creativity can be spiritually and financially rewarding. Frequent unusual, secretive or sudden romantic or sexual opportunities tend to arise.

Empty Eighth House Pisces

This individual can be emotionally secretive, sensitive, shy and withdrawn. Matters regarding death, sexuality, the occult and finances acquired through others can be a source of worry or fear. Secretive joint financial ventures are likely, however losses through the marriage or partnership are not ruled out. Indecision, confusion or deception can also bring financial or spiritual setbacks. There is interest in the mysteries of life and faith in the unknown. Intuition can border on psychic ability. Extra precautions should always be taken when near water as well as with gasses, liquids, alcohol, drugs and medication.

Neptune is the ruler of this empty house. If positioned in the ninth, travel, law, religion, philosophy, spirituality, higher knowledge or education is likely of interest. The intellect is intuitive, impressionable and visionary. Financial gain may come through teaching, studying, long distance travel and publishing.

If Neptune also forms a trine with Mars, the intellect is energetic and creative. Intuitive, imaginative or inspirational ideas and impulses can easily be put into constructive action. There is the ability to sense danger, particularly while in foreign lands or among others of different cultures. This is a good aspect for a dancer.

Eighth House Ruler

Regardless of the sign or ruling planet, we will briefly go through the ruler of the empty eighth house as it may be positioned throughout the remaining 11 houses. Always consider the aspects formed with this planet as it provides the necessary information as to determining whether these energies are beneficial or challenging.

The ruler of the empty eighth house found in the ninth indicates that foreign contacts or dealings can affect finances. Foreign investments are likely and wealth can be achieved through matters related to travel, education, law, publishing, advertising, religion, and philosophy. Long journeys can be spiritually intense and emotionally transforming. The intellect is penetrating, resourceful, suspicious yet optimistic.

The ruler of the empty eighth house found in the tenth shows the tendency to be involved in a career where research or the handling of other's finances is likely. Psychology, death related professions, sexuality and investigation might also be careers of interest. There can be the element of secrecy surrounding the career or reputation. An inheritance is likely to come from the parent represented by this house.

The ruler of the empty eighth house found in the eleventh indicates secretive hopes and dreams. Financial ventures may be entered with friends or group organizations. Participation in secret organizations or clubs can be of interest. The element of secrecy and suspicion tends to cloud intense friendships. The death of a friend may be profound and transforming.

The ruler of the empty eighth house found in the twelfth increases the tendency of being a private and secretive individual. Emotions run deep and fear of death and the occult is likely. Intuition is enhanced with this placing. This is a good position for financial research and investigation, however money acquired through others can be a source of fear, worry or self-undoing. Secret physical relationships are likely to attract.

The ruler of the empty eighth house found in the first indicates that the native is strongly secretive, sexual and mysterious. This is the image projected to others. Matters dealing with death, sexuality and the occult can be of particular interest. Through personal efforts and contacts is the native able to prosper financially. Many rebirths or personal transformations throughout the life are experienced.

The ruler of the empty eighth house found in the second shows that the individual places much importance is acquiring finances and material possessions. Self-worth and security is measured by the wealth accumulated, however it may go as easy as it comes. There is ability to make money work for others. Financial goals can be realized through matters related to insurance, legacies, wills, death and sexuality.

The ruler of the empty eighth house found in the third reveals a quick and inquisitive mind when it comes to matters related to death, sexuality, the afterlife and the occult. An astute mentality is evident and can be an asset when handling or acquiring finances from others. An inheritance may come from a sibling, same generation relative or neighbor.

The ruler of the empty eighth house found in the fourth increases the tendency toward family or domestic secrets and mysteries. An inheritance may come from a family member or the parent represented by this house and may come in the form of land, home or property. There can be interest in financial investments or transactions involving land, real estate or a family relative.

The ruler of the empty eighth house found in the fifth brings an active romantic life, as physical needs are strong. Younger partners are often selected. An inheritance may come from a past lover. Gambling, investing or speculating with other's finances may be of interest. Investing in sports, entertainment, theater, teaching, children, hobbies and games is likely. Creative urges are highly energetic. Mystery or secrets may involve a child or children.

The ruler of the empty eighth house found in the sixth shows that the individual is drawn to work or performing services that involve the finances of others. This is a good placing for a financial researcher, analyst, investor or banker. There can be an element of secrecy involving co-workers or the work place. Worrying over health, the job, death, sexuality and taxes is evident.

The ruler of the empty eighth house found in the seventh indicates that the marriage or partnership can affect the financial status. This can be a good placing for a lawyer, counselor or financial advisor. An inheritance may come from a spouse or partner. Physical desires are strong and important within these relationships. This placing often indicates secrets involving the marriage or partnership.

Empty Ninth House

The ninth house answers questions regarding the higher mind, mental exploration and further education. It also governs over foreign connections, dealings, languages, long distance travel, law, religion, spirituality, philosophy, publishing and advertising. The planetary ruler of this house when empty, is analyzed by the position and aspects formed to other planets. The aspects describe the potential or challenges within this department of life.

Empty Ninth House Aries

This individual is enthusiastic and energetic when it comes to higher learning and developing new ideas on life. Travel brings excitement whether physically or mentally. The native can be emotionally impulsive or aggressive regarding legal matters, spirituality, education, religion, law, politics and philosophy. The intellect is sharp, quick, alert and independent of thought. There is a tendency toward being active, outgoing and daring coupled with a love of adventure. Exploring foreign cultures, languages and lands are of particular interest. Impulsiveness while traveling can bring accidents as more chances tend to be taken when abroad.

Mars is the ruler of this empty house. If found in the seventh, travel and long-term relationships provide much excitement. A marriage or partnership is likely formed with a foreigner or during a long distance trip. Arguments are to be expected while traveling or within the marriage or partnership. Joint financial dealings are handled in a rapid and impulsive manner. Legal matters should be cautiously approached before taking hasty action.

If Mars also forms a trine with Mercury, the native possesses a high level of intellectual energy. Learning powers and concentration skills are well developed. The mind is resourceful, active and capable of inspiring others. This aspect benefits teachers, writers, lawyers, politicians, publicists and the mastering of foreign languages.

Empty Ninth House Taurus

This individual can be stubborn and persistent when it comes to higher knowledge, education, philosophy, religion or spirituality. Views and opinions are not easily changed, as beliefs are consistent and carefully thought out. Finances are likely acquired or improved through foreign contacts, projects or ventures. Self-indulgences while traveling are often experienced.

Venus is the ruler of this empty house. If positioned in the eleventh, friends of a different culture or nationality are likely. There are often ties to clubs or organization of foreign backgrounds. Long distance travel with groups or friends is often experienced. Romance and friendships are often encountered with foreign individuals or while abroad. A friend may become a spouse or partner and may share the same philosophical beliefs and education as the native. Hopes and dreams are likely related to spiritual matters, religion, travel, foreign cultures, law, publishing or higher education. Friendships often include musicians and artists.

If Venus also forms a conjunction with Saturn, the individual often attract friends that are different in age or more established and secure in life. Saturn may restrict or inhibit emotional expression, particularly with friends, females, romantic partners, foreigners or while abroad. However, lasting and meaningful ties can be established and maintained within these relationships.

Empty Ninth House Gemini

This individual enjoys conversations and debates over spiritual, religious, political, foreign or philosophical ideas and matters. The tendency to be mentally vacillating or skeptical is also probable. The mind is restless, alert, curious and inquisitive. Travel, whether mentally or physically, is of particular interest.

Mercury is the ruler of this empty house. If found in the sixth, the native is suited to work involving radio, magazines, reporting, education, law, travel, research, writing, publishing and the mastering of foreign languages. The job may involve foreign products or co-workers from other lands and may result in frequent long distance travels.

If Mercury also forms a square with Neptune, the tendency to excessive worry is emphasized. A lack of concentration or clear and honest communication can bring problems at work or while traveling long distance. Daydreaming can also prove to be costly at the work place. Extra caution is suggested when traveling by water or swimming in foreign waters as well as entering into agreements while abroad, with co-workers or with those of different nationalities. It is particular important for this native to be honest with co-workers and those of foreign cultures.

Empty Ninth House Cancer

This individual possesses an emotionally philosophical or religious mind. Interest in such topics as history, archaeology, real estate, family heritage and foreign languages is likely. The intellect is imaginative, changeable and intuitive. Knowledge is easily absorbed and memory is well developed. Frequent travels by water or across oceans are evident. The mother may be of foreign birth. A home in a place far from birth is likely established. It is important for the native to instill moral and spiritual values in the family.

The Moon is the ruler of this empty house. If positioned in the first, a restless and caring nature is evident. Spiritual or philosophical ideas and beliefs can be fluctuating and inconstant. The native may project an image of spirituality and sympathy. Inspiration can be attained through imagination and intuition. There is a tendency to rely mostly on gut feeling rather than intellectual reason.

If the Moon also forms a trine with Jupiter, the native is generous, popular, optimistic, outspoken and good humored. There is a strong sense of justice, fairness and altruism that is projected to others. Success can be achieved through dealings with foreign natives, cultures or projects involving foreign lands. A profession involving law or religion can also be rewarding. Family ties are strong and domestic issues predominate. This is a fortunate placing and aspect for travel, particularly long distance.

Empty Ninth House Leo

This native possesses high aspirations and believes that knowledge is power. Ideas are grand and the intellect is strong and fixed. There is dynamic interest in furthering education and travel can also be a great source of enjoyment. This individual is optimistic and tolerant of other's political, philosophical or spiritual views.

The Sun is the ruler of this empty house. If found in the fourth, a comfortable home is likely established in a place far from birth and most likely during the second half of life. Family ties are strong even if a residence is established abroad. The native feels at home among foreigners and their cultures. The parent ruled by this house is likely of a different birthplace or nationality. This placing is conducive to teaching from the home.

If the Sun also forms a trine with Saturn, the nature is kind, sincere and reliable. Morals and powers of concentration are well developed, as is organizational ability. Ideas pursued must have a practical goal. Ambitions can be fulfilled through patience, determination and hard work. Benefits are likely to arise through travel, real estate, law or politics. This is a good placing for higher learning, as constructive mental development is evident. This aspect tends to indicate longevity; however it is emphasized when the Sun is in this house. Success during the second half of life is almost assured.

Empty Ninth House Virgo

This individual has practical and rational ideals as well as highly organized thoughts. However, philosophical or ideological concepts are often regarded with skepticism.

The mind is studious, inquisitive, analytical and enjoys solving problems. There is a marked ability to study, research and debate for endless hours. Long trips are planned efficiently down to the last detail. Frequent travel due to education, health or work related reasons are likely. Travel can also bring learning experiences.

Mercury is the ruler of this empty house. If found in the second, financial gains through publishing, law, writing, lecturing, advertising, broadcasting, education, religion and spirituality are evident. A flair for business and salesmanship is also likely. Money can also be acquired through foreign contacts and dealings with other lands bringing in two sources of income. Financial affairs are planned and handled in a detailed and methodical manner. The mind is constantly searching for methods and ideas that can bring wealth.

If Mercury also forms an opposition with Saturn, financial ventures with foreigners or dealings involving other lands can bring heavy responsibilities and setbacks. Finances can be a source of worry, sorrow or discouragement. Financial loss can also arise through personal ideals and beliefs. This individual can be argumentative particularly regarding matters related to religion, law, politics, philosophy, spirituality, higher knowledge, the occult and foreigners. There can be suspicion and disagreements with those of other cultures.

Empty Ninth House Libra

This individual is morally just and refined but can be indecisive and easily influenced, particularly regarding spirituality, politics, the occult, religion, law and philosophy. Good perception and a sense of balance however, are evident. A marriage or partner may be of a foreign background or encountered while abroad and much pleasure is derived through travel and studying foreign cultures. This placing is often found in the charts of judges and lawyers.

Venus is the ruler of this empty house. If positioned in the fifth, many romantic partners are likely of different cultures and can be encountered through travel or within institutions of education. The tendency to be over-indulgent and indecisive while on vacation is pronounced. This is a good placing for teaching, particularly children as ruled by this house, as well as professions related to the publishing industry, entertainment and stock market. Venus in the fifth house often indicates and represents a female child.

If Venus also forms a square with Neptune, the native may have difficulty with decision-making abilities. Deception and miscommunication can arise through speculative financial ventures, romantic partners, particularly those of foreign cultures, or those encountered in other lands. It is important for the native to get all the facts before dealing with such issues, as there is a tendency to be easily misled in these areas. Self-indulgences or escapism can bring serious setbacks, especially while traveling or on vacation. Daydreaming often involves lands far away or ideal romantic relationships. The tendency towards being overly sensitive or self-sacrificing within romantic relationships is evident.

Empty Ninth House Scorpio

This native is passionate and emotionally intense regarding beliefs, ideals and personal opinions. Mysterious or obscure philosophies and ideologies can be a source of fascination or interest. The individual is highly inquisitive and curious regarding the mysteries of life. Spiritual or religious beliefs can bring an awakening or personal transformation. The intellect is deep, penetrating and resourceful. When it comes to furthering education and higher knowledge, there is much determination, ambition and tireless energy. Secretive situations or behind the scenes events are likely to arise while traveling. There is often a marked level of suspicion of the motives of those of other cultures.

Pluto is the ruler of this empty house. If found in the tenth, the career likely involves travel, advertising, publishing, education, publishing, law, foreign contacts or business. The career may take the individual to foreign countries. Professional ambition and drive to succeed is powerful. Spiritual leadership can manifest as a result of deep insight into human behavior.

If Pluto also forms a trine with the Sun, the native is self-confident and well respected by others, particularly within the career. This is a good placing for an employer, as the character is powerful, determined and courageous with a great capacity for leadership. The career itself may provide personal transformation. Secrets can also be related to the profession.

Empty Ninth House Sagittarius

This native possesses high ideals and is capable of great intellectual inspiration. The personality is outgoing and adventurous and the outlook on life is expansive, jovial and optimistic. There is tolerance for the ideals of others and a flair for languages is likely.

Ties to foreign lands or individuals are evident as there is a marked interest in travel and different cultures. Spirituality and higher learning are also of particular interest. This is a good placing for teaching as well careers related to publishing, lecturing, traveling, philosophy, law, advertising, religion or foreign interests and businesses.

Jupiter is the ruler of this empty house. If found in the third, success in the fields of writing and communication is likely. Interests are primarily intellectual as curiosity and thirst for knowledge is indicated. Benefits are likely to arise through the furtherance and pursuit of higher knowledge. The intellect and manner of speech is enthusiastic, humorous and optimistic. Frequent short and long trips will likely be experienced.

If Jupiter also forms a square with the Moon, obstacles or arguments with siblings, same generation relatives, foreigners or females in general are likely and particularly while traveling. Being overly optimistic and emotionally excessive can also bring setbacks.

Controlling emotional impulses and financial extravagances is recommended. Over-indulging while on vacation or in foreign lands can prove detrimental.

Empty Ninth House Capricorn

This individual has a rational and conservative approach toward intellectual or philosophical matters and discussions. However, new or innovative ideas are viewed in a skeptical manner as traditional outlooks and thoughts are respected and better understood. The intellect is serious, deep and well grounded. The ability to study is well developed and good concentration skills are evident. Goals and ambitions can include travel, foreign cultures and furthering education. Increased responsibilities may also arrive from these sources.

Saturn is the ruler of this empty house. If found in the eighth, financial gains are likely acquired through established or older individuals, particularly from other cultures. Financial responsibilities are well handled. Only safe and secure investments are of particular interest, even if the rewards materialize in later years. Foreign investments can bring slow and steady gains.

If Saturn also forms a sextile to Mercury, this individual possesses great logic and reason, especially when it comes to handling finances acquired through others. The intellect is disciplined, cautious and moralistic. Powers of concentration and organizational ability are well developed. This placing is often found in the charts of teachers, lecturers, mathematicians and writers.

Empty Ninth House Aquarius

This native is intellectually independent, unorthodox, innovative, highly inspired and open to new ideas. The mind is original, active, idealistic, inventive and curious. There is an altruistic attitude in regards to those of foreign cultures or races. Sudden travel opportunities are likely to arise and unusual or exciting situations may develop during long distance trips. This is a good placing for radio or television broadcasting.

Uranus is the ruler of this empty house. If positioned in the twelfth, the native can spiritually benefit from healing others. There is a strong interest and attraction to the unusual, unconventional and to mystical beliefs. Frequent periods of solitude and introspection are often sought. This placing tends to increase intuition and psychic ability. Matters related to law, politics, religion and travel may be handled secretly or behind the scenes. Hospitalization or incarceration while in distant land is not ruled out.

If Uranus also forms a trine with Mars, the intellect is energetic, ingenious, constructive and alert. Decision-making skills are well developed. Any traits of intellectual impulsiveness can be put to good and practical use. This placing favors careers related to electricity, surgery, the military, sports, computers and aviation.

Empty Ninth House Pisces

This individual is somewhat intellectually shy or secretive. The mentality can be can be indecisive, intuitive, imaginative and impressionable. Worry, fear or anxiety may develop through matters related to travel, law, mysticism, spirituality, religion and philosophy. This placing often indicates devotion to a religious or spiritual cause. Escaping to foreign lands or through foreign cultures, studies or languages is of particular interest. Traveling overseas or to places near water can bring a sense of calmness. However, there can be confusion, misunderstandings or deception while abroad or through foreigners.

Neptune is the ruler of this empty house. If found in the sixth, the work may take the native on long distance trips or is perhaps involved in the travel industry. Intuition can pay off at work. Many jobs such as those related to law, religion, spirituality, travel, liquids, gasses, the sea, water, healing, medication, art, dance, music, publishing or teaching can bring rewards. There is great sensitivity to co-workers and job environment or surroundings.

Worry, indecision or fears may affect the health. Illness while in foreign countries may frequently develop, particularly involving infections or poisoning. Foreign foods can be harmful to the health and all drugs or medication should carefully be taken, especially in foreign lands.

If Neptune also forms an opposition with the Moon, trouble or loss through employees or subordinates is likely, particularly those female. Travel by water or to a place near water can bring obstacles and delays and even hospitalization as the Moon is in the twelfth house of confinement. There is the possibility of self-deception and adverse escapist tendencies. Self-indulgences are especially harmful with this aspect. Health can be delicate, particularly to the stomach region. Much care is advised while in foreign lands in regards to money-making schemes and political or religious associations as this individual is subject to deception within these areas. This is the aspect of the dreamer. There is danger in self-delusion or being victimized. Emotions, the mother, a woman, or a co-worker can bring trouble or loss particularly while furthering education or travel. Secrets, betrayal or deception between others or at work are likely. It could affect the health. The native may be self-deluded or victimized at the workplace. Jealousy, deception and unreliability can bring misunderstanding and breakups with co-workers or foreigners. Being mislead or misinterpreted by others, particularly females, should be watched for.

Ninth House Ruler

Regardless of the sign or ruling planet, we will briefly go through the ruler of the empty ninth house as it may be positioned throughout the remaining 11 houses. Always consider the aspects formed with this planet as it provides the necessary information as to determining whether these energies are beneficial or challenging.

The ruler of the empty ninth house found in the tenth indicates that a career in a country other than birth, or professional dealings with foreigners are likely. Higher learning plays a big part in the native's profession, achievements and goals. This placing is conducive to careers involving travel, publishing, foreign cultures or contacts, advertising, publishing and law as well as diplomats, spiritual and religious leaders.

The ruler of the empty ninth house found in the eleventh reveals a tendency to make friends while abroad or encounter friendships among foreigners. Spiritual friends are likely to attract and traveling with groups, organizations or friends is evident. The native's hopes and dreams are tied to spirituality, higher learning, education or travel. Foreign or cultural clubs or associations are of particular interest.

The ruler of the empty ninth house found in the twelfth shows the possibility of behind the scenes activities involving travel, spirituality, religion or law. Secret enemies may be foreigners or encountered abroad. This placing benefits teaching mystical or occult subjects as well as psychology and counseling. Secretive encounters while on long-distance trips are likely to occur.

The ruler of the empty ninth house found in the first increases the need to expand the personality through higher learning or spiritual matters. Personal qualities are best expressed through institutions of higher learning or the furthering of education. Much fondness for study and philosophy is likely. Religious or philosophical beliefs are independent of thought and strongly pronounced.

The ruler of the empty ninth house found in the second indicates the tendency toward financial and material gain through matters related to publishing, travel, foreign business or connections. Benefits are also likely through education, law, philosophy, religion, spirituality and the pursuit of higher knowledge.

The ruler of the empty ninth house found in the third brings pronounced learning ability, intense curiosity and thirst for knowledge. Many languages can easily be mastered. The manner of communicating can be philosophical and optimistic. Travel is of particular interest, whether mentally or through long or short distance trips. This placing is conducive to matters related to education, writing, advertising, transportation, publishing and communication.

The ruler of the empty ninth house found in the fourth shows a tendency toward having a residence or owning property in a foreign land, particularly in the later years. People of other cultures are welcomed into the native's home and family. Foreign objects likely adorn the home.

The ruler of the empty ninth house found in the fifth increases the tendency toward encountering romance with foreigners or while traveling abroad. Romance may also be found through institutions of learning. This placing often indicates one who teaches children. Much enjoyment and pleasure is derived from travel, spirituality, religion or study.

The ruler of the empty ninth house found in the sixth indicates that work must provide mental freedom and the chance to explore. Co-workers are likely to be foreigners or the job involves foreign business or cultures. Work may take this native abroad and traveling with co-workers is also likely. This placing is conducive to writing, teaching, traveling, legal work and publishing.

The ruler of the empty ninth house found in the seventh reveals that the spouse or partner may be encountered while traveling abroad or through institutions of learning. The spouse or partner is likely of a different nationality than the native. Open enemies or competitors may be among those of other cultures. Frequent travel with the spouse or partner is evident.

The ruler of the empty ninth house found in the eighth brings the likelihood of being involved in foreign investments. An inheritance may come from a foreign source. Secrets and mysteries may surface when traveling or dealing with foreigners. Higher learning can bring a sense of personal renewal and transformation.

Empty Tenth House

The tenth house answers questions regarding social status, career, life's calling, ambitions, aspirations, reputation and honors. It also represents the employer, influential people of power and the parent not ruled by the fourth house. The tenth house often contains the highest point in the chart known as the Midheaven and indicates the type of career best suited. The planetary ruler of this house when empty, is analyzed by the position and aspects formed to other planets. The aspects describe the potential or challenges with this department of life.

Empty Tenth House Aries

This individual is highly ambitious and impulsive when it comes to the career and professional matters. A competitive, courageous, aggressive and outgoing reputation is evident. There is leadership potential, as positions of authority are easily handled. An active career is likely as a tremendous amount of energy is channeled into professional goals and aspirations. The career must provide challenges or competition as boredom can easily set in. This placing is often found in the charts of security guards, law enforcers, military soldiers, butchers, dentists, motivators, executives, firemen, mechanics, carpenters, athletes, wrestlers, butchers, welders and surgeons.

Mars is the ruler of this empty house. If found in the fourth, professional gains are likely achieved through jobs involving land, real estate, property or domestic services and products. A career may develop through working from the home. There can be conflicts of interest or sources of arguments regarding the home, career and responsibilities. A parent is likely domineering and argumentative or has Aries prominent.

If Mars also forms a trine with Jupiter, this individual possesses much energy and enthusiasm, particularly in the career and family life. A good relationship and strong bond with the parent ruled by this house is likely. Expansive ambitions can help set the foundation for an active and pleasant home life. This placing favors professions involving sports, travel, adventure and spiritual or religious work as the personality is self-confident, optimistic, kind and generous.

Empty Tenth House Taurus

This native is determined and patient toward career matters and professional ambitions. The personality is persistent, reliable and loyal, particularly in the career area. Energy in this area tends to only be expended in matters that will bring a useful and practical outcome. Finances acquired through reputation or career are often spent on luxury items.

This placing is often found in the charts of artists, musicians, singers, antique dealers, Realtors, designers, dress makers, jewelers, florists, decorators and gardeners.

Venus is the ruler of this empty house. If found in the first, the individual appreciates beauty and is highly aware of self-image. This image projected to others is likely one who is wealthy, career-minded or professional. Career matters are dealt with in a practical and rational manner. Professional success comes from personal efforts, persistence and patience. As an employer, the native can be popular, friendly and somewhat charming. However, there is a fondness for flirting with professional contacts, connections or through the career.

If Venus also forms a square with Saturn, the native may have to make sacrifices in the romantic or career area as these two areas can interfere with each other. Emotional frustrations can arise through the profession. The tendency to be self-absorbed, shy or selfish is not ruled out. The parent ruled by this house can be a source of worry or responsibility.

Empty Tenth House Gemini

This individual is attracted to careers involving communication, business, publishing, journalism and writing. The versatility of this sign enables the native to also succeed in broadcasting, accounting, telemarketing, transportation, messenger industry, sales and the media. The profession chosen must provide variety and mental stimulation as boredom can quickly set in. Conversations tend to revolve around the career and professional goals. There is ability to communicate well with those in power or higher authority. As Gemini is a dual sign, the possibility of having two occupations is likely. This individual may excel at teaching and public speaking, as well as in a career requiring skilled hands and dexterity.

Mercury is the ruler of this empty house. If positioned in the third, intellectual work is the key to a fulfilling professional life as success can be found through careers requiring mental skill and an active and alert mind. The career may involve commuting short distances. This is a good placing for occupations related to research, study, writing, lecturing or communication in general.

If Mercury also forms a square with Neptune, there is the tendency to over-worry or be indecisive about career issues. As the nature is highly communicative, there is danger of being misinterpreted, deceived or confused, particularly in the career. Verbal indiscretion and incorrect information can bring setbacks to career or during short distance trips. Lack of concentration can also be detrimental to the profession. Conversations with the parent ruled by this house can be vague, misleading, lacking in truth or frequently misunderstood. This individual should avoid any kind of deception or schemes as the reputation may suffer.

Empty Tenth House Cancer

This native is attracted to professions involving the caring of others such as nursing and healing. Other careers may involve domestic products or services, real estate and the hotel and restaurant industry. The career may be fluctuating due to a restless professional nature. As an employer, good business sense and intuition is evident. Family heritage and reputation is closely guarded. This placing is also often found in the charts of individuals who work in construction, architecture or farming.

The Moon is the ruler of this empty house. If found in the second, financial help or gains are likely to come from a family member or parent. Financial goals are often set, as the native believes that wealth brings status. Fluctuations with income are evident and may affect the reputation. The nature can be security-oriented and financially tenacious.

If the Moon also forms a sextile with the Sun, the native can enjoy rewarding career opportunities and a solid professional reputation. This placing often brings recognition, fame, wealth or strong family ties. There is balance and harmony between the emotions and ambitions.

Empty Tenth House Leo

This native is ambitious, competitive and has leadership potential. Goals are pursued with confidence and managerial abilities are well developed. There is a strong will to succeed in the profession as well a need for approval, respect, power and social status. As an employer, the image projected is one of self-confidence, honor, trust, and dignity. This placing is often found in the charts of actors, politicians and social leaders as being in the spotlight is easily handled. Other vocational possibilities include entertaining, the fashion or jewelry industry, counseling, public relations, advertising, the stock market or any position of authority.

The Sun is the ruler of this empty house. If positioned in the eleventh, faithful friends can help advance career and social goals as the friendships chosen are generally of high social or professional status. Hopes and dreams revolve around goals and vocational ambitions. Popularity among peers is likely as the native is a team player. The career may involve social ties or group organizations. The parent ruled by this house can be a good friend.

If the Sun also forms a square with Uranus, erratic or unstable friendships may disrupt professional goals and dreams. It would be highly beneficial to learn how to adjust to changes, obstacles and challenges within the career as well as with friendships. Sudden, unusual or unexpected circumstances can frequently occur among friends or within the career.

Empty Tenth House Virgo

This individual is detail minded, discriminative, analytical and emotionally reserved within the career. As an employer, the image projected is one of efficiency and discreetness. The work place must be orderly, clean and tidy with everything in meticulous order. The ability to easily adjust to routine and a set schedule within the career is pronounced. The native is highly selective regarding career choices and matters. There is attraction to professions in the health, veterinary, medical, hygiene and service industry or any career that requires intellectual skills and discrimination. As the personality is highly detail-oriented, this placing is often found in the charts of analysts, critics, editors, teachers, writers, statisticians, technicians, researchers, accountants, mathematicians and office managers.

Mercury is the ruler of this empty house. If found in the fifth, the native can succeed in careers related to sports, the entertainment industry and the stock market. This is also a good placing for teaching children, as good communication with young people is evident. Artistic or creative talents can be successfully applied to the vocation. Romance can be formed through career ties or encountered within and may involve a superior or boss. The parent ruled by the tenth house is likely to be fun-loving and young at heart. Movies or games that challenge the mind are often selected.

If Mercury also forms a trine with Pluto, the intellect is clear, resourceful and alert. This aspect brings great capacity for concentration, will power and research that can be successfully applied to the vocation. This personality is not easily fooled as getting to the truth of a matter is of great importance. When the native speaks, it can leave quite an impact upon others. There is a tendency to form passionate and physically intense romances with those of higher authority or power that are usually initiated or encountered within the career.

Empty Tenth House Libra

This individual has a diplomatic, sociable and likeable reputation. Cordial and pleasant relations with employers are evident as there is talent for charming people of authority. The vocational environment should be harmonious, pleasant and stress-free. As an employer, there is a tendency toward relying upon the advice of others and seeking their approval before making professional decisions. Indecision and indolence may also hinder career progress. An attraction to professional partnerships is likely. The spouse may be involved with or encountered through the career. A career involving interaction with the public is likely of interest and work involving manual labor is generally avoided. This placing is often found in the charts of fashion designers, hairdressers, musicians, artists, jewelers, cosmeticians, judges, mediators, diplomats, lawyers and marriage counselors.

Venus is the ruler of this empty house. If positioned in the twelfth, the reputation is likely to be somewhat shy and introverted. Secrets may surround the career or involve places of confinement such as hospitals and prisons or may include behind the scenes activities. Career goals can be realized through secretive means or contacts. Healing, counseling, psychiatry and related fields tend to attract. Clandestine relations with employers or those of authority are likely of interest. The parent ruled by this house may hold many secrets.

If Venus also forms an opposition with Saturn, relationships involving the career should strongly be guarded, as they may not be what they appear. Frustrations through self-imposed limitations, personal sacrifices or vocational fears may prevent professional success. A romantic relationship, marriage or partnership may damage the reputation or bring career setbacks. The profession may limit or decrease romantic or marriage opportunities. The business or marriage partner is likely of a considerable age difference.

Empty Tenth House Scorpio

This individual is emotionally intense and resourceful regarding the career, goals and ambitions. A profession involving secrecy, the occult or any form of mysticism is likely to attract. There is a tendency to be suspicious of employers and those in positions of authority or power. A promotion may result through the demise of another. As an employer, the native must be in total control and can be driven, competitive and ruthless. This placing is often found in the charts of surgeons, athletes, soldiers and law enforcers as well as psychologists, detectives, life insurance dealers, politicians, law enforcers, morticians, militants, surgeons and researchers.

Pluto is the ruler of this empty house. If found in the sixth, there is a powerful bond or strong hold over employees and co-workers. As an employer, the tendency to dominate those of lesser positions of authority is evident. Promotions within the job can be frequent and bring a sense of renewal or personal transformation. This placing is often found in the charts of those involved in work related to public services or health matters. The parent ruled by this house can be somewhat fussy and critical.

If Pluto also forms a trine with the Moon, the native possesses tremendous will power, emotional intensity, courage and determination, both within the career and on a daily basis. Creative talents should be explored within the work place as it could lead to a promotion and professional success. Female co-workers can further status or professional ambitions and goals. Occupations involving real estate, domestic products or the service, restaurant or hotel industry are likely to attract.

Empty Tenth House Sagittarius

This individual requires a career that can provide excitement, a sense of independence and exploration. The tendency toward having high aspirations and an optimistic outlook are evident when it comes to the pursuance of goals and ambitions. Careers related to foreign cultures, sports, religion, education, languages, the travel industry and the outdoors are likely to attract. Many publishers, explorers, professors, politicians, translators, librarians, judges, travel agents, priests, teachers and philosophers have this placing.

Jupiter is the ruler of this empty house. If found in the seventh, professional success and goals can be achieved through a marriage or partnership. The choice of partner may be encountered through the career or can be of a different age, cultural background or public standing. This relationship may be formed on the basis of achieving status or professional success. Many lawyers, counselors, advisors and mediators have this placing. The parent ruled by this house has a good sense of humor, is optimistic and generous.

If Jupiter also forms a sextile with Uranus, the native often experiences fortunate changes, surprises and opportunities within the career, reputation, marriage or partnership. This individual possesses a wealth of originality and personal magnetism that can be used to further marriage and professional goals. This is an excellent placing for an astrologer.

Empty Tenth House Capricorn

This native is private, reserved and conservative when it comes to career goals. The reputation is closely guarded and the nature is highly ambitious. Organizational and managerial skills are well developed. Professional ambitions are approached with great caution and determination. Perseverance, patience, and self-discipline are the keys to success that are likely to come later in life. However, these goals and ambitions can ultimately lead to a lonely or isolated existence. This individual is able to accept great responsibilities with the career. This placing favors careers in politics, banking, architecture, farming, sales, real estate, archaeology, dentistry, big business, government, law and civil or military service.

Saturn is the ruler of this empty house. If found in the ninth, the lengthy pursuit of higher education can greatly benefit the reputation, career or professional goals. The native is able to apply great concentration and serious discipline in pursuing education and career goals. High aspirations are evident when it comes to achieving these goals. Connections formed with foreigners or older individuals can bring benefits to the career and reputation. Traveling to foreign lands for career or education matters is likely to attract. This placing is often found in the charts of religious leaders, publishers, explorers and teachers.

If Saturn also forms an opposition with Mercury, losses, delays and miscommunication are likely to arise during long distance travels, particularly those related to the career or the pursuit of a higher education. Discouragement and pessimism within the career can hinder progress. The reputation may suffer as a result of being argumentative, defensive or suspicious of foreigners and those in positions of authority. Much caution should also be applied when speaking to others of a different background or when involved in conversations regarding foreign cultures and individuals.

Empty Tenth House Aquarius

This native requires a career that is somewhat unusual, unconventional, different or exciting. As routine is not easily handled, independence, originality and freedom within the profession are also sought. The reputation can be somewhat offbeat or eccentric. Goals and ambitions tend to be different from the norm or are approached in an unorthodox manner. Friends can be instrumental in shaping the native's ambitions, career or reputation. This placing is conducive to careers related to computers, aviation, science, astrology, electronics, television, radio, psychology and charity or social work. Many pilots, sociologists, engineers, machinists, astronomers and inventors also have this placing. The parent ruled by this house is somewhat inspiring, unpredictable and sociable.

Uranus is the ruler of this empty house. If positioned in the eighth, financial gains acquired through others can further the reputation or professional goals. This placing is conducive to career related to death, taxes, banking or any profession that deals with other's finances. A sudden inheritance or financial windfall may arise through unusual or unexpected sources. Unconventional beliefs are held when it comes to matters related to sexuality, death and the occult.

If Uranus also forms a square with the Moon, the native may experience losses through big business deals or as a result of mismanaging the funds of others. Changes of fortune may also arise through unwise decisions or unexpected circumstances involving corporate finances, insurances, taxes, inheritance, and marriage or business partnerships. These financial setbacks may damage the reputation and status. Arguments with females within or as a result of the career are evident. The home and family life may be disrupted by career choices. Professional setbacks and financial fluctuations can bring increased nervousness and emotional mood swings.

Empty Tenth House Pisces

This native is private and introverted, particularly when it comes to professional matters and ambitions. As an employer, there is much sympathy toward others as well as the tendency to overworry. Intuition and imagination can be used to further career goals. Many sacrifices within the career are indicated and as Pisces is a dual sign, it is not uncommon with this placing to have two professions. The career must provide a creative or artistic outlet. Many actors, artists, musicians, fantasy or romance writers, poets, dancers, pharmacists, nurses, bartenders, psychologists and photographers have this placing. A career involving the sea, liquids, chemicals, gasses, healing arts, clairvoyance or the film industry is also likely to attract. The parent ruled by this house is compassionate, introverted and devoted.

Neptune is the ruler of this empty house. If found in the first, what is projected to others is not necessarily the true and real personality within. This placing is conducive to actors that are constantly role-playing. It is important for the native to project an artistic or mysterious image through the profession.

If Neptune also forms a trine with Mercury, the intuitive faculties are greatly enhanced, as are creative, imaginative and artistic talents. These are the tools and skills that can bring professional goals closer and help achieve the reputation desired. There is great sensitivity to those in position of higher authority. Many writers of romance, fantasy, fiction or mystery have this placing.

Tenth House Ruler

Regardless of the sign or ruling planet, we will briefly go through the ruler of the empty tenth house as it may be positioned throughout the remaining 11 houses. Always consider the aspects formed with this planet as it provides the necessary information as to determining whether these energies are beneficial or challenging.

The ruler of the empty tenth house found in the eleventh indicates that friendships can be formed through the career. Friends can also be instrumental in achieving professional goals, as the choice of friends tends to be among the older, wealthy, influential and more established natives. Hopes and dreams are strongly linked to the career. The native's reputation can be formed or at least influenced by group associations and friendships. The native can be popular among peers and well liked within the career. The parent ruled by this house can also be a good friend.

The ruler of the empty tenth house found in the twelfth reveals a tendency to select a career that is behind the scenes, performed in seclusion or within places of confinement. Secrets or mysteries may surround the career and hidden enemies are likely to result. Covert contacts can also influence the career or reputation. This placing is conducive to psychologists, analysts, healers, counselors and any work requiring research and investigation. The parent ruled by this house may have many secrets and be quite introverted and shy.

The ruler of the empty tenth house found in the first increases the need to project the personality and individuality through the career as a professional reputation is of great importance. There is great ambition projected to others and a strong interest in career matters. Professional success and goals can be achieved through personal efforts and may be realized early in life. This placing is conducive to being one's own boss.

The ruler of the empty tenth house found in the second indicates that professional goals are motivated by wealth and security needs. Self-worth and reputation is measured and established through the career. It is imperative for the native to project an image of wealth, as financial status is highly relevant. A career related to finances is likely to attract. Finances may be increased through the parent ruled by this house.

The ruler of the empty tenth house found in the third brings the tendency to be involved in a career related to communications or any profession requiring a sharp intellect. It is through mental skills that the reputation can be established. Many speakers, teacher and writers have this placing. The career may take the native on frequent short trips or require the need to commute back and forth.

The ruler of the empty tenth house found in the fourth reveals the tendency to select a career related to agriculture, farming, domestic products or services, land, property or real estate. Archaeology, antiques and family ancestry are likely of interest. The family and career are linked or conflict with one another. The native feels quite at home within the career and a profession may be established from the home.

The ruler of the empty tenth house found in the fifth shows the possibility of working in a career where creativity and self-expression is essential. A hobby can be turned into a profession. Romantic connections are likely to arise and formed with older individuals or are encountered through the career. This placing is also conducive to working with children, the stock market, sports, entertainment and the sports industry.

The ruler of the empty tenth house found in the sixth increases the need to be of valuable service within the career. The profession chosen may involve a service performed for others. The native may rise within the career and govern over those who once were co-workers. Routine within the career is well handled however; the tendency to overwork should be avoided as the health may suffer. This placing is conducive to working with animals, healing and medicine.

The ruler of the empty tenth house found in the seventh indicates the likelihood of forming a professional partnership with another. The spouse or partner may be encountered within the career. This placing may also reveal that the native is married to the career. Many competitors or open enemies are involved within the profession. This is a good placing for a mediator, counselor, lawyer, advisor or work involving public relations.

The ruler of the empty tenth house found in the eighth reveals the possibility of being in a career involved with research, death, taxes, sexuality, other's finances or mysteries and the occult. The career may bring a sense of renewal and personal transformation. The reputation can be one of secrecy, sexuality, allure or mystery.

The ruler of the empty tenth house found in the ninth shows the likelihood of being in a career related to spirituality, travel, higher learning, law, philosophy, publishing, advertising, the media or foreign cultures. The career may take the individual to foreign lands and connections with those of other cultures can influence the career or reputation. Acquiring a higher education can strongly benefit the career and bring such goals closer to fruition.

Empty Eleventh House

The eleventh house answers questions involving the native's hopes, wishes and long-term goals. It also represents friends, clubs, social and group activities or associations. The planetary ruler of this house when empty, is analyzed by the positions and aspects formed to other planets. The aspects describe the potential or challenges within this department of life.

Empty Eleventh House Aries

This individual leads an active professional life and enjoys spending time with friends. There is interest in participating in clubs or organizations with friends or associations related to the career. The ability to lead in group activities or social circles and causes is evident. Goals and aspirations are enthusiastically and actively pursued. There is no fear or hesitation in accepting challenges or initiating projects or friendships. Often, there is a sense of constant competition among friends or peers. Impatience and sudden actions can end friendships or prevent the realization of hopes and wishes.

Mars is the ruler of this empty house. If found in the fourth, friends can interfere or disrupt the home or family life. Domestic quarrels can also arise due to the native's involvement or participation in social causes or group organizations. Friends are always welcomed in this individual's home although they can be a source of family disagreements. The family can be instrumental in helping the native achieve hopes and dreams. Close relatives or the parent ruled by this house can be considered a friend.

If Mars also forms a conjunction with Pluto, a tremendous amount of energy is expressed within the domestic circle and among friends or group organizations. There is a strong desire to assert the personality among friends and family members. The tendency to dominate in these areas can alienate and bring quarrels and disagreements. As a group leader, the ability to influence friends and relatives with the power of suggestion or force is evident.

Empty Eleventh House Taurus

This native attracts and seeks friendships that are loyal, reliable and enduring, however, there is the tendency to being somewhat possessive and thrifty among friends. Self-indulgences are often experienced among friends or group organizations. Friends may also be financially well off or are able to help in the attainment of goals and wishes, particularly if related to finances. Participation in associations related to money, music, art, luxury or beauty items can be of interest. Hopes and dreams are rational, practical and pursued slowly with patience and determination.

Venus is the ruler of this empty house. If in the second, finances can be closely linked to friendships, causes or group associations. The possibility of mixing finances with friends or organizations is evident. Money can be a motivating factor for forming friendships or belonging to clubs or associations. Financial benefits may come through these social connections or organizations.

If Venus also forms a trine with Saturn, good business sense can be applied to the furthering of social causes or financial goals. Friendships, romance and group ties can be loyal and enduring. Romance with older individuals can be encountered through friends or group connections. The choice of friends is often among those of a considerable age difference.

Empty Eleventh House Gemini

This native selects friendships of the intellectual, literary and communicative kind. Friends can also be unreliable, fickle or changeable and are often of a younger age. Debates, conversations and exchange of ideas are frequent among friends and group organizations. Hopes and wishes are often a topic of conversation among friends and the tendency to gossip is not ruled out. This placing is conducive to group speaking.

Mercury is the ruler of this empty house. If found in the seventh, the spouse or business partner can become a good friend. Friendships and partnerships formed are based upon intellectual rapport and mutual thinking. The social life of the marriage or partnership is active with many friends or group ties. Often, the spouse or partner is younger in age. Communications are especially important for the native to maintain an important relationship. A friend may become a spouse or partner or the spouse or partner will become or remain a friend. This placing is conducive to group leaders, public speakers as well as professions involving law, sales, public relations, literature and counseling.

If Mercury also forms an opposition with Jupiter, the native may experience obstacles within the marriage, in lawsuits or group associations and organizations. There is a strong need to carefully consider entering into any contractual agreements before making final decisions. The tendency toward exaggeration or bending the truth should strongly be avoided in order to prevent frequent quarrels or misunderstandings with friends, spouse or partners. Promises should carefully be made, as they are not often fulfilled. Over-optimism or over-generosity can ruin a friendship, partnership, marriage or prevent hopes and dreams from coming true. Friendships can interfere within the marriage or partnership.

Empty Eleventh House Cancer

This individual forms friendships and group associations based on emotional and security needs. There is a tendency to be faithful, nurturing and over protective of friends, however, there is also danger of clinging to these associations or being somewhat tenacious or needy. The ability to be intuitive of friends is evident as the intellect can be highly sensitive to their thoughts and opinions. When hurt by a friendship, this individual retreats into a shell. There is nothing this native would not do for a friend in need. Friends are likely to be inconstant and changeable, although through them, close emotional ties are sought. Friends are treated like family members and a relative, particularly the mother, can become a good friend.

The Moon is the ruler of this empty house. If found in the sixth, friendships are likely formed with co-workers or established at the work place. There is a tendency to socialize with co-workers or belong to a group or association related to the job. Friends can be instrumental in helping the native find work, however, many jobs or frequent changes within are indicated. This placing is conducive to working with friends, particularly in the health, hotel, restaurant, domestic or service industry.

If the Moon also forms a sextile with Neptune, intuitive skills are well integrated with the emotional self. Work-related goals can be realized by trusting gut feeling and hunches. The imagination is powerful and many creative employment opportunities requiring this talent may arise. Psychic bonds with special friends are likely established as well interest in organizations related to mysticism or spirituality. This placing is conducive to working as clairvoyants, bartenders, healers, pharmacists, veterinarians, nurses, photographers, dancers, musicians, artists and actors.

Empty Eleventh House Leo

This individual is somewhat competitive among friends and within social groups or activities. Fun times are often spent with good friends and group organizations. There is ambition and leadership potential that can be used in such relationships and organizations. The tendency to be somewhat too trusting and bossy or demanding of friendships is likely, however you will not find a more loyal friend. The friends chosen are equally loyal yet young at heart, creative, influential or very popular. Help and support from friends may come at a time of need.

The Sun is the ruler of this empty house. If found in the third, much time is spent communicating with friends, siblings or same generation relatives. The intellect is active and highly creative. This is a good placing for a public speaker or social leader, as there is a strong need to communicate thoughts, knowledge or ideas to friends, organizations and groups of people. Many short distance travels are likely experienced with friends, siblings or as a result of group ties and social causes or organizations.

If the Sun also forms a trine with Uranus, the native is able to come up with worthwhile ideas that are inspiring and innovative to others. There is considerable talent in organizing and managing group or social activities. The native possesses much intelligence, leadership ability and personal magnetism that easily attracts and wins friends.

Empty Eleventh House Virgo

This individual can be somewhat shy and introverted among friends and within group associations or organizations. Friendships can be formed with co-workers or encountered through the job. Discrimination is applied when selecting or forming friendships as there are high standards regarding what a friend should be. It is essential to have intellectual compatibility with friends in order for them to last, however the tendency toward criticizing and faultfinding can severe these ties. Finding or securing work can also be accomplished through friendships, clubs or societies. There is ability to manage and organize social groups, causes or societies.

Mercury is the ruler of this empty house. If positioned in the tenth, participating in societies, clubs or organizations can enhance the reputation or improve social standing. Friends can also be highly instrumental in helping career matters. Socializing with co-workers is likely of interest as well as being a member of a group, club, cause or organization related to the profession. The choice of friends often includes peers, older or more established individuals or tend to be formed through the career. The native's hopes and dreams are related to professional goals and are likely career-oriented. There is talent and ability for professions that involve communication, travel or writing. This is a good placing for a representative or speaker of a particular group or organization.

If Mercury also forms a square to Pluto, the individual should control the tendency to gossip, speak unfavorably or dominate friends and others within group settings. Friendships can be formed on the basis of achieving power or furthering career goals. The manner of communicating, particularly to friends and within the career, can be hurtful if not controlled and could end up alienating others. Suspicious tendencies can be experienced among group associations or within friendships.

Empty Eleventh House Libra

This individual has many friends, leads a sociable life and is popular among groups and clubs. The types of friendships that are formed tend to be among the refined, attractive, artistic or cultured as emphasis on status and appearance is important. There is a tendency to be easily swayed or influenced by friends or group associations. Hopes and dreams may be realized through a partnership or relationship that first begins as a friendship or turns into a special friendship. There is interest in social or artistic organizations and societies through which romances and friends can be encountered.

Venus is the ruler of this empty house. If positioned in the ninth, the individual if fond of traveling with friends and partners. Romance and friendships can be formed within institutions of higher learning, with those of different cultures and religions or are encountered while traveling abroad. The marriage or partnership may begin as a special friendship or can be introduced by a friend or within a group or organization. Studying languages, spirituality or foreign cultures can be of particular interest.

If Venus also forms a trine with Saturn, lasting and meaningful friendships and relationships are likely formed. Older individuals or those more established in life are often chosen as friends or romantic partners. Relationships are treasured and never taken for granted, as the nature is to be a loyal, faithful and dependable friend, spouse or partner.

Empty Eleventh House Scorpio

This native tends to form emotionally intense relationships with strong, powerful and dynamic individuals. These associations can be secretive or prone to jealousy, suspicion and revenge. Strong opinions and extreme emotions shared with friends can terminate such relationships. Physical relationships can easily be formed with friends. There are reformist tendencies that can be applied within societies, groups or organizations. Hopes and dreams are intense and emotional and when it comes to making wishes come true, this individual can be most resourceful and determined.

Pluto is the ruler of this empty house. If found in the first, many changes and personal transformations in life are likely encountered through friendships or group settings. There is an ability to experience a sense of rebirth through such associations and contacts within. The personality can be driven, intimidating and powerfully projected onto others, particularly to friends and within clubs or societies. This placing is indicative of a powerful group leader that can intensely project ideas and beliefs upon friendships as well as among group settings, organizations or associations.

If Pluto also forms a sextile with Mercury, the native is able to verbally express the intellect and ideas in a most commanding and effective manner. The mind is restless, adaptable and changeable, however, capable of great concentration and persuasion. This placing is conducive to a group leader among friends as well as a speaker within organizations and societies. Hopes and dreams are often communicated to friends and groups or clubs.

Empty Eleventh House Sagittarius

This individual appreciates honesty and good times among friends. Much enjoyment is derived from adventure, exploration, sports, outdoor activities and travel, particularly with friends or in group settings. Friendships are often formed with foreigners and participation or interest in cultural groups or societies can be of interest. The tendency toward generosity is evident with friends or social organizations and causes. Optimism and a well-developed sense of humor attracts many friends and social invitations.

Jupiter is the ruler of this empty house. If found in the eighth, interest in occult matters can be shared with friends, groups or associations. Physical relationships are likely established with friends, or met through a club or group setting, or are introduced by friends. Traveling with friends or groups can also bring opportunities for physically romantic encounters. Financial opportunities can arise through friendships or through the death of a friend. Investing with friends, in associations, or an organization can also bring monetary gain.

If Jupiter also forms a square with Mars, the native may exhibit erratic behavior among friends or within group activities. The tendency toward rebelling or crusading for a group or cause is likely. Exaggeration and promising more than can be delivered can severe friendships or group ties. Financial recklessness, over-generosity, blind optimism and impulsive gambling can bring heavy setbacks. Financial transactions among friendships may not yield desired results. Other's people's money may be wasted due to personal, extravagant needs or due to social or religious causes and organizations.

Empty Eleventh House Capricorn

This native may select friends or belong to groups and organizations that can further career ambitions or enhance the status and reputation. Social ties and friendships are often formed with older, influential, career-oriented, hard-working and more established individuals, however few they may be. Friends can bring extra responsibilities or are instrumental in attaining hopes and dreams related to security needs and social status. Friendships and group ties can be enduring but somewhat lacking in warmth or emotion.

Saturn is the ruler of this empty house. If found in the fifth, romance is often found with friends or introduced through friendships and group connections. Romantic relationships may sever due to interference from friendships. Older romantic partners are sought and interest in pleasure or entertainment may be minimal. It is not easy for this native to let loose and have fun. There is difficulty in showing emotions or expressing feelings to friends, romantic partners, children, or within group organizations and associations. Children, however few, can bring heavy responsibilities or prevent friendships from developing.

If Saturn also forms a trine with the Moon, female friends can be of considerable benefit to the native when it comes to furthering romantic goals. Responsibilities are well handled, particularly those involving children and friendships. Romance can be found with an older friend or through established organizations or causes. A romantic partner may also become a valuable friend. The mother or a female can help in attaining dreams and wishes. The relationship with the mother can be regarded as a close, enduring friendship and strong ties can be formed with children.

Empty Eleventh House Aquarius

This individual may have an abundance of friendships but they are kept at arm's length, as the nature is somewhat detached yet sociable and friendly. It is essential to have intellectual compatibility with friends as opposed to emotional. The choice of friends is among the eccentric, unusual or bohemian type of people. Friendships may begin as suddenly as they can end. Interest in social causes or humanitarian groups and organizations is evident. The native works well in group situations. Hopes and dreams can be somewhat unconventional.

Uranus is the ruler of this empty house. If found in the twelfth, intuition is greatly enhanced and can be used to understand friendships and further dreams and wishes. Surprising, unusual conditions and clandestine pacts likely surround the friendships formed. The types of friends that are attracted tend to also be introverted and secretive. Friends can also be influential or responsible for the native's self-undoing. This placing can bring a fear of forming close emotional ties with friends. There is interest in secret or behind the scenes organizations and clubs.

If Uranus also forms a square with Mars, friendships can be argumentative, unstable or unreliable. These associations can be a frequent source of emotional upset or betrayal. Secrets can be revealed or uncovered resulting in sudden severed ties. Arguments or disagreements tend to arise, particularly with male friends. This placing suggests applying much caution in physical activities, especially those that involve friendships and organizations or clubs. Discredit or unrealized hopes and dreams may arise through friendships or as a result of participating in radical or unconventional groups or organizations.

Empty Eleventh House Pisces

This individual seeks deep, devoted and lasting friendships or ties to organizations. There can be behind the scenes or deceptive activities related within, as interest in mysterious, secretive or occult associations is evident. The native can be somewhat shy in approaching friendships or participating in groups. The tendency toward being super- sensitive and easily influenced or imposed upon by friendships or groups is likely. Self-sacrifice for a friendship or cause is not ruled out. The types of friends attracted are spiritual, highly intuitive, artistic or escapists. There can be much compassion and idealism in regards to humanity. This placing indicates a dreamer who enjoys escaping with friends or into a world of private hopes and wishes.

Neptune is the ruler of this empty house. If found in the second, finances can be affected by friendships or group causes and organizations. Wealthy friends and financial ties are of particular interest and secretive or unusual sources of income are evident. There is danger of squandering money on organizations and friendships or being taken advantage of financially by dubious friendships or ties to causes or associations.

If Neptune also forms a trine with Venus, intuition can be used in increasing finances and attracting friends. Romantic ties can develop with or through friends. The native seeks ideal companions, whether social or romantic. Financial gain can be attained through friendships and creative talents or connections.

Eleventh House Ruler

Regardless of the sign or ruling planet, we will briefly go through the ruler of the empty eleventh house as it may be positioned throughout the remaining 11 houses. Always consider the aspects formed with this planet as it provides the necessary information as to determining whether these energies are beneficial or challenging.

The ruler of the empty eleventh house found in the twelfth indicates that friends can turn into secret enemies or become the cause of self-undoing. Fears or sorrows can be related to friendships, group organizations or hopes and dreams. There is much intuition and compassion when it comes to friendships. The tendency toward forming secretive associations or friendships is likely and a strong need to escape among group ties or with friends is indicated.

The ruler of the empty eleventh house found in the first shows that the individual is friendly and attracts friends easily. Personality is also inventive, original, and can be rebellious. Sudden changes are often experienced. This placing tends to bring a personal interest in humanitarian issues. The native best expresses the personality through friendships and groups or clubs.

The ruler of the empty eleventh house found in the second reveals the tendency toward increasing or depleting finances through friendships, group ties or club affiliations. The native can be possessive of friends and wealthy associations can be of particular interest. Self-worth may be measured through friendships and alliances. Hopes and wishes are tied to finances and material possessions.

The ruler of the empty eleventh house found in the third increases the need to communicate within friendships and group ties. This is a good placing for a group speaker or writer. Friendships are formed upon intellectual and communicative compatibility. Siblings, same generation relatives and neighbors can also become good friends. Hopes and dreams are often communicated within these relationships. Short trips are often taken with friends.

The ruler of the empty eleventh house found in the fourth shows that friends are welcomed or entertained in the home and are treated as family. Meetings related to groups, clubs or causes are often held at the native's home. This placing attracts many friends as roommates. Hopes and wishes are family-related and relatives as well as the parent represented by this house can become good friends.

The ruler of the empty eleventh house found in the fifth indicates that the individual tends to become friends with romantic partners or these partners end up being good friends. Good times and much fun can be enjoyed with friendships or within group affiliations. The types of friends attracted are fun, exciting, creative and outgoing. Children can also be among the native's friends. Hopes and wishes are related to romance or children.

The ruler of the empty eleventh house found in the sixth reveals that friendships are formed with co-workers or encountered through the work place. Friends can also interfere within the work environment. Participation in organizations or clubs related to the job can be of particular interest. There is likely much daily contact with friends or group affiliations.

The ruler of the empty eleventh house found in the seventh increases the likelihood of forming a marriage or partnership with or through a friend. Friends can be among competitors, advisors or open enemies. The marriage or partnerships consists of many friends or ties to social groups and humanitarian causes. Hopes and dreams are related to the marriage or partnership.

The ruler of the empty eleventh house found in the eighth shows an interest in occult or secretive organizations or cults. Friendships may be secretive or financially motivated. This is a good placing for one who handles the finances of an organization or cause. Physical relations with friends are not ruled out. Money can be gained through a friend or by participating in a club or society.

The ruler of the empty eleventh house found in the ninth brings the need to further education through group organizations or societies. Friends can be made through institutions of higher learning. Friendships are also formed with foreigners or while visiting another country. Much enjoyment can be derived from traveling with friends or in groups. Foreign cultures or studies and humanitarian causes are of particular interest. The types of friends chosen are among the spiritual, intellectual or philosophical.

The ruler of the empty eleventh house found in the tenth reveals the need to further the career or reputation through friends or group alliances. Friends are mainly related or encountered through the career. The types of friends chosen are older, established and influential, particularly to the profession and reputation. Hopes and dreams are tied to the career or social standing. The parent ruled by this house is also a good friend.

Empty Twelfth House

The twelfth house answers questions involving the subconscious mind, past life memories, karma, fears, escapism, and dreams. Places of confinement or seclusion also fall under this house. It also represents psychology, research, self-undoing, limitations, secrets and sorrows. This is the house most difficult to tap into as it deals with the subconscious mind. As the seventh house answers questions related to open enemies such as competitors or rivals, the twelfth house reveals information regarding secret enemies. The planetary ruler of this house when empty, is analyzed by the position and aspects formed to other planets. The aspects describe the potential or challenges within this department of life.

Empty Twelfth House Aries

This native enjoys activities and actions that are behind the scenes or secretive in nature. New projects or ideas can secretly be initiated and implemented. Impulsive or hasty decisions and actions however, can bring a sorrow or a sense of defeat. The subconscious mind is motivated by action, energy and desires.

Mars is the ruler of this empty house. If found in the fifth, there can be a strong attraction to secretive romantic involvements that are subconsciously motivated or initiated. Romance can be encountered through institutions or places of confinement. There can also be a fear of romantic relationships or of being a parent.

Self-undoing may come through romance or children as it is the native's karma to experience lessons related within these relationships. Escaping through romance, children or creative activities is likely of interest. Impulsive gambling or financial speculation can bring losses or confinement. This is a good placing for a child psychologist.

If Mars also forms a trine with Pluto, subconscious actions can bring a sense of renewal and transformation. There is a tremendous amount of positive energy that the native can draw upon when needed. Ability to sense danger can be present and courage can be among the individual's many hidden talents.

Empty Twelfth House Taurus

This individual enjoys retreating into a quiet and private world where creative talents can be explored, such as music and art. Material losses can be a source of worry and fear of poverty is evident. A subconscious desire for wealth and material possessions may bring the native's self-undoing. Money can come from secretive or behind the scenes activities or sources. Habits or patterns from the past may be hard to break. Self-indulgences may deplete finances.

Venus is the ruler of this empty house. If found in the ninth, the individual enjoys escaping the realities of life by traveling into foreign lands or exploring different cultures, whether physically or mentally. Secretive romantic alliances may be formed with foreigners or while abroad. Fear of travel, flying or of people from different cultures is likely. A love of solitude is coupled with a need for furthering education. This is an excellent placing for studying, research and religious or charitable work. The lessons involved in this life involve exploring and expanding the intellect.

If Venus also forms a square with Saturn, the individual may suffer financial losses as a result of a romance or connections with foreigners. Financial responsibilities may interfere with romance or the pursuance of higher knowledge. Clandestine financial agreements or investments can bring restrictions, obstacles or losses. Shyness may prevent the native from accomplishing romantic goals.

Empty Twelfth House Gemini

This individual is able to speak openly and communicate emotions, fears and sorrows. The subconscious mind is active, restless, and flexible. Mental faculties are strongly motivated by past subconscious memories and habits. Intellectual creativity is evident and much thinking is done in solitude. There is a tendency toward revealing secrets and over-communicating can be a source of self-undoing or loss. Work in seclusion or behind the scenes activities related to communication, writing or the media are of interest. This placing often indicates shyness when it comes to public speaking. The native can be prone to talking in sleep.

Mercury is the ruler of this empty house. If positioned in the second, financial gain is likely through secretive associations or behind the scenes activities. Creative and literary talents or interests can bring wealth. This is a good placing for a writer of mystery or the occult. The karmic lessons involve finances, material values and possessions. A lack of self-worth or fear of poverty, financial loss and security can bring the native's self-undoing.

If Mercury also forms an opposition with Pluto, finances can be affected by transactions involving mystical, secretive or spiritual organizations. Nervous tension is evident and is likely brought on by financial issues. The subconscious mind can prompt verbal outbursts and extra tact should always be applied when communicating. Finding ways to release tensions arising from private and deep thoughts can bring a sense of inner calmness.

Empty Twelfth House Cancer

This individual possesses a highly emotional, receptive and sensitive subconscious mind. There is a tendency to escape into an imaginative private world. Moods can be motivated or inspired by the subconscious. Fears and sorrows are often related to domestic issues, the family or the mother. This placing indicates great sensitivity to the opinions of family members. Feelings of self-pity, guilt or insecurity should be controlled. The native's karma is the family and domestic responsibilities or relationships.

The Moon is the ruler of this empty house. If found in the fourth, the domestic life can be inconstant, changeable, highly sensitive or extremely private. Family losses can be devastating as the tendency toward being over-protective of family members is evident. There can be fear of the parent ruled by this house that stems from childhood years. Secrets tend to surround a parent, family member or the domestic environment. The home can be a place of soul searching, contemplation and spiritual or emotional comfort, particularly if situated near a body of water.

If the Moon also forms a trine with Jupiter, a kind and generous natures brings popularity within family members. A large family is likely. Phobias and sorrows can be handled in an optimistic and healthy manner. Financial luck can be realized through dealings with real estate, agriculture, land, domestic products, family members or the hotel and food industry and particularly during the second half of life.

Empty Twelfth House Leo

This individual does not enjoy being in the spotlight as the tendency is toward being retiring and introverted. Creativity is best expressed in places of seclusion and during moments of privacy and solitude. However, there is leadership potential that can be applied in secretive or behind the scenes activities or involvements. This is placing is often found in the charts of actors, entertainers and performers. The native's karma involves romantic relationships or children.

The Sun is the ruler of this empty house. If positioned in the eighth, interest in mysteries and hidden or occult subjects are likely of interest. Secrets and sorrows are often experienced through financial dealings with others, particularly with insurances and tax matters as well as inheritances and legacies. Secret and physical romantic affairs are often attracted. A fear of death or sex is not ruled out.

If the Sun also forms a sextile with Neptune, the imagination and level of intuition is well developed and can be used to further financial goals. Any activity requiring creativity, inspiration, musical or artistic talents can also help bring financial and spiritual goals closer. There is a tendency toward escaping into the imagination or within physical romantic relationships.

Empty Twelfth House Virgo

This individual is shy, modest, introverted and private. Subconscious thoughts are well organized and minutely analyzed. Sorrows and fears are likely kept closely guarded. The tendency toward being highly critical and worrisome can bring losses or self-undoing. The intellect is sharp and talent in research and studying is evident, particularly where great attention to detail is required. Secret enemies may arise from the work place. This placing often indicates hospitalization at some point in life. The native's karma involves work and services performed for others.

Mercury is the ruler of this empty house. If found in the third, writing can be a great outlet for any intellectual creativity that needs to be expressed or for problems that need solving. The ability to write or speak about such matters as psychology or the occult is evident. The native is much more talkative when the ruler is found here. The subconscious mind is active and meditation can be especially rewarding, as high-strung tendencies are evident. Secrets involving the work or siblings and same age relatives are not ruled out. Karma may also be related to communication within these family relationships.

If Mercury also forms a square with the Moon, frequent arguments are likely to arise with females, the mother or while traveling short distances. Gossip can turn others into secret enemies. Fears stemming from the past or childhood may interfere with the health or intellectual progress and clarity. This placing increases nervousness to the extent that it could bring stomach disorders. Emotions and intellect are often in conflict with each other. There can be a tendency toward being over-sensitive and indecisive, particularly if Libra rises.

Empty Twelfth House Libra

This native is highly sensitive to outer forces and perhaps easily influenced. Indecision and inertia can bring losses, sorrow or self-undoing. There can be a fear of being alone or of places of confinement. There is a tendency to escape harsh realties through relationships, music, art or literature. Artistic and creative inspiration stems from the subconscious. Secret partnerships may be of interest. The spouse or partner may be encountered in places of seclusion or confinement.

Venus is the ruler of this empty house. If positioned in the tenth, social or artistic goals are evident. A marriage, important relationship or partnership may enhance the career, reputation and status. The profession may involve secrecy, behind the scenes activities or places of seclusion and confinement. Secrets may also surround the parent ruled by this house. This placing brings much popularity and increases the chances of professional success. However, fear of superiors or those in high authority may deter progress. This individual's karma involves relationships, the career and ambitions.

If Venus also forms a conjunction with the Moon, cultural or artistic connections, particularly female, can further career goals and enhance the reputation. This is a good placing for a career requiring artistic and creative talent, as there is great appreciation for beauty, harmony and balance. A close bond with the mother is evident. Indulgences should be avoided as a means of escape.

Empty Twelfth House Scorpio

This individual can be suspicious, jealous, vengeful or unforgiving of enemies. These negative feelings of resentment tend to be kept within and may bring sorrow and self-undoing. The subconscious mind can be emotionally intense and motivated by deep feelings. In the face of hardship, there is courage and determination. This placing favors research and investigation or a career in psychology.

Pluto is the ruler of this empty house. If found in the seventh, the ability to clearly perceive partners is evident. It is not easy to be fooled by others, as there is incisive intuition that can be used within relationships. The tendency toward dominating or escaping through partnerships can bring sorrow, losses or self-undoing. Secrets tend to involve the marriage or partnership, however these relationships may bring a profound emotional change or a deep and personal transformation. The native's karma involves marriage and important relationships. A fear of deep emotional commitment or relationships is likely experienced.

If Pluto also forms an opposition with Mars, arguments and aggressiveness can bring losses to important relationships. Personal commitments with others can be volatile and prone to power struggles. It is crucial to consider other's feelings in order to prevent frequent quarrels, particularly within the marriage or partnership. The need to dominate within these relationships should be minimized and controlled. A tremendous sense of inner strength and will power is evident.

Empty Twelfth House Sagittarius

This individual enjoys escaping into a world of religious studies, travel, foreign cultures or the mysteries of life. Sorrows and fears can be handled in an optimistic manner, however naiveté or misplaced faith can bring losses or self-undoing. This placing is known to bring a sense of protection from secret enemies. A fear of travel is not ruled out.

Jupiter is the ruler of this empty house. If found in the sixth, the need to serve, guide and heal others can be strong. Work involving charities, behind the scenes activities, psychology, research and places of confinement such as hospitals or prisons, are likely of interest. This is a good placement for spiritual healing or counseling. Such fields as law, religion, travel or publishing are also likely to attract. Secretive elements tend to surround the work place and clandestine relationships with co-workers are not ruled out. The native's karma involves work and health. The need to overindulgence as a means of escape from worries, sorrows or fears can bring serious health setbacks. This placing often indicates psychosomatic illnesses.

If Jupiter also forms a trine to the Sun, good deeds can be greatly rewarded. The native enjoys fine health and good luck. Cordial relations with co-workers and subordinates are indicated. Job opportunities abound, as the native is a popular, optimistic, generous and humorous with co-workers. A positive working environment is sought where there is room for exploration and solitude. Not only is there protection from enemies but from danger as well.

Empty Twelfth House Capricorn

This individual enjoys spending time in privacy and seclusion. Subconscious fears can bring setbacks, sorrows and limitations. Pessimism, lack of self-confidence and a persecution complex may result in self-undoing. Feelings of loneliness and depression are taken very seriously and can deter progress. However, hidden inner strengths can be drawn upon in times of need. The tendency toward making sacrifices is evident and through discipline, hard work and perseverance, can achievements be realized.

Saturn is the ruler of this empty house. If found in the eleventh, interest in social organizations or those of a secretive or occult nature are likely of interest. Secretive friendships are often attracted, particularly with older, career-oriented or more established individuals. There can be a fear of forming close friendships or involvement in groups or associations due to a deep-seated need for privacy. Friends may be few but are lasting and faithful, however at some time a friend may prove to be a secret enemy. This native's karma is friendships, as lessons in this area require experiencing. Only through persistence, effort and determination can hopes and wishes be fulfilled.

If Saturn also forms a square with Mercury, sacrifices, duty and responsibilities are likely brought upon through friends and dealings with associations or organizations. The native can be demanding and distant within friendships and frequently experience misunderstandings. Legal matters involving friendships or associations should carefully be examined. Restrictions are self-imposed and may result from subconscious fears and thoughts. The tendency to over-worry can be particularly detrimental. There can be difficulty in expressing feelings as emotions are closely guarded. When it comes to public speaking, shyness can hinder progress.

Empty Twelfth House Aquarius

This individual possesses an emotionally independent or detached subconscious. Forms of mysticism or occult and secretive associations can be of considerable interest as there is a psychological or subconscious attraction to the unusual and innovative. The ability to deal with fears through acute intuition can bring spiritual well being. A fear of forming close friendships or group ties is likely as distinguishing friends from enemies may come with a certain level of difficulty. Unexpected and sudden obstacles or enemies can be encountered, particularly within group associations and friendships. The native's karma is important friendships and relationships within.

Uranus is the ruler of this empty house. If positioned in the first, an inventive, unique, inspiring and creative subconscious and personality are evident. Hidden aspects within the subconscious mind may require attention. A mysterious or secretive image is projected, as there is a tendency to hide a part of the personality from others. A constant desire for change and excitement is often experienced, as the native is restless, dynamic and somewhat rebellious.

If Uranus also forms a trine with the Moon, a constant desire for change and excitement is often experienced, as the personality is restless and rebellious. New opportunities and the unconventional or unusual are often sought. Frequent changes of residence are likely. Domestic ties can be harmonious, yet somehow unorthodox or unusual. Intuition, creativity and imagination are highly developed and can be drawn upon for emotional and spiritual well-being. Female friends are likely attracted and a strong bond with the mother is evident. This is an excellent placing for an astrologer or psychologist as there is an ability to tap into the unknown, intuition and the subconscious.

Empty Twelfth House Pisces

This individual has a powerful subconscious, imagination and intuition. Frequent periods of solitude and introspection can bring inner peace. Escaping within the imagination or through self-indulgences is likely. Subconscious fears can bring sorrow, obstacles or self-undoing. The tendency to worry about self-imposed fears is evident. The native's karma is spiritual growth.

Neptune is the ruler of this empty house. If found in the fifth, secret romances are likely attracted. There can be deception or illusion regarding such relationships. Much caution is needed when speculating financially or gambling as it could bring losses and sorrow. Escapism is often experienced through romances or creative projects and activities. Much appreciation of the theatre, cinema and places of amusement or gambling is evident. Children, particularly those sensitive and intuitive, can be a great source of worry or fear. This placing is conducive to teaching occult or mystical subjects.

If Neptune also forms a sextile to Mars, imagination and intuition are highly active, energetic and put to good constructive use. The desire to take action is well integrated with the subconscious mind. Creative and intuitive impulses stem from the subconscious.

It is not easy to fool this individual as intuition provides much inner guidance. Good relations with children are evident. The pursuit of secret romances is of particular interest. This placing is often found in the charts of dancers and performers.

Twelfth House Ruler

Regardless of the sign or ruling planet, we will briefly go through the ruler of the empty twelfth house as it may be positioned throughout the remaining 11 houses. Always consider the aspects formed with this planet as it provides the necessary information as to determining whether these energies are beneficial or challenging.

The ruler of the empty twelfth house found in the first indicates that the native projects an introverted, secretive and private persona. Time spent alone is frequently sought. Fears and sorrows may be self-imposed. Sensitivity and intuition is highly developed. Outer influences and other's emotions can strongly influence or affect the personality and well-being. Self-deception is to be avoided as well as the tendency toward escapism.

The ruler of the empty twelfth house found in the second brings financial gains or losses through secretive or behind the scenes activities or involvements. Secretive financial ventures should carefully be examined and considered. There can be a fear of poverty or financial and material loss. Sorrow and self-undoing may come about as a result of finances.

The ruler of the empty twelfth house found in the third shows that the native communicates in a passive and introverted manner, however keeping secrets may not come easy. The imagination and subconscious mind is strong and active. The intellect is perceptive and intuitive. There can be a secret or psychic bond or link with a sibling or same generation relative. This is a good placing for researching or writing fiction as well as occult or psychological subjects.

The ruler of the empty twelfth house found in the fourth reveals a tendency toward family or domestic secrets. A secret may also involve the birth. Fears may stem from childhood or family issues. Emotions are strong and intuition can be useful particularly within family matters. The parent ruled by this house may have a secret or is prone to escapism and self-indulgences. A quiet, peaceful home is desired where frequent moments of seclusion and meditation are enjoyed. Karmic lessons are experienced through the family.

The ruler of the empty twelfth house found in the fifth indicates many secretive and romantic relationships that are subconsciously initiated. Escaping through romance or gambling is evident. Clandestine financial opportunities should carefully be considered. Creative talent is likely. Secrets or sorrows may arise through children. Intuition can be of considerable benefit when dealing with children or romantic partners. Karmic lessons are experienced through romance and children.

The ruler of the empty twelfth house found in the sixth shows that work in seclusion or behind the scenes can be of special interest. Jobs in hospital, prison, charity or healing work are likely to attract, as there can be a strong need to heal, serve, counsel or guide others. Co-workers can be secretive or deceiving. The tendency to over-worry about the health matters can bring psychosomatic illnesses.

The ruler of the empty twelfth house found in the seventh increases the chances of secrecy or behind the scenes activities within a marriage or partnership. A secret marriage is not ruled out. The spouse or partner may be intuitive, introverted and compassionate. This individual may be encountered within a place of seclusion or confinement. Competitors and rivals may be more than open enemies. There can be a fear of marriage or close emotional commitments.

The ruler of the empty twelfth house found in the eighth indicates that secrets or deception may be related to inheritances or financial gains through others. Physical relationships of a clandestine nature are likely to attract. This placing brings interest in occult or esoteric subjects. Talent for research and study is indicated. There is likely a fear of death or sexuality.

The ruler of the empty twelfth house found in the ninth indicates a profound intellect and need to pursue higher learning. Moments of quiet solitude and study are often sought. Interest in spirituality and escaping through foreign cultures or countries is likely. Enemies may be foreign or encountered abroad. Hidden elements may surface while in a foreign country. This is a good placing for student or publisher of fiction and the occult.

The ruler of the empty twelfth house found in the tenth shows that the native is attracted to a career that is behind the scenes or spent in seclusion. A fear of superiors or those of higher authority is evident. There can be secrets involving the profession and reputation. Self-imposed fears and limitations can prevent ambitions from being fulfilled. A subconscious need to improve the status is strong. The parent ruled by this house is likely intuitive, introverted or an escapist.

The ruler of the empty twelfth house found in the eleventh brings the tendency toward forming secretive or behind the scene friendships. A fear of forming close friendships is not ruled out. Intuitive and compassionate friends are attracted. The native is not above sacrificing for a friend. Delusion and sorrow may arise through friendships. The tendency toward escaping through friends or group ties is evident. Friends are attracted that are psychic, compassionate, artistic or escapists. This placing is known to indicate that these are the same friends from a previous life. Involvement with occult or secretive organizations can be of special interest. Hopes and dreams are kept privately within and can provide a means of escape.

Case Studies

Madonna

Madonna's first empty house is the fifth. Saturn ruling this house indicates few or no offspring. However, it also indicates the tendency towards experiencing motherhood at a late age. Madonna became a mother at age 38, and then again five days before her 42nd birthday. At age six, Madonna experienced the loss that natal Saturn can bring in the fourth house when her mother died of cancer. At this time her progressed Moon, representing the mother, traveled through her fourth house of family, sorrow and endings, thus triggering Saturn's influence. Progressed Mercury, her chart ruler, formed a conjunction with Pluto bringing death and transformation to her life.

Her first child was born when transiting Venus formed an exact conjunction with the Moon. The Moon and Venus are feminine by nature and a baby girl named Lourdes was born October 14, 1996. Transiting Jupiter through her fifth house of children also formed a trine with the Moon and Mars. Transiting Pluto was also applying to form a conjunction with her fourth house cusp representing family issues. This event filled the void that Madonna felt since here mother's death. In other words, the sorrow that Saturn brought in the fourth house of family was remedied through its ruling empty fifth house of children. Madonna has stated that she has found herself through her children that have finally made her life complete.

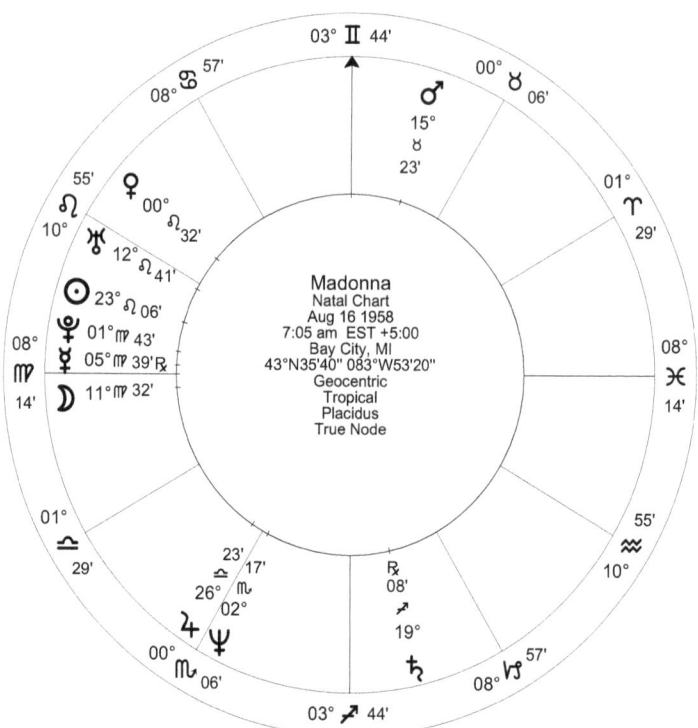

Madonna: August 16, 1958, 7:05 a.m., Bay City, Michigan
Source: Lois Rodden's AstroDatabank.

Madonna's empty seventh house is ruled by Neptune. Pisces, ruler of Neptune, is a dual sign and tends to bring more than one marriage. Madonna married Academy Award winner and fellow Leo, Sean Penn on the day of her 27th birthday. At this time, progressed Venus formed a sextile with Neptune, ruler of the empty seventh house triggering the event. Progressed Venus also formed a conjunction with Pluto, dispositor of Neptune. It is interesting to note that Neptune rules actors.

Madonna is currently married to her second husband, British film director, Guy Ritchie. As indicated in the seventh house chapter, Pisces and the opposite sign Virgo, are favorable long-term romantic compatibility. Ritchie was born a Virgo on September 10,

1968. There is great compatibility when one's Sun sign is the same sign as the other's Ascendant as Madonna is Virgo rising.

During her 41st/42nd year, the progressed Sun formed a trine with the Midheaven indicating a change in status and parenthood. It was at this time that they had a child together and settled down in marriage. Further triggering this event was progressed Mars as it applied to form a conjunction with the Midheaven. The Sun and Mars are masculine by nature and a baby boy named Rocco was born August 11, 2000. When Madonna married for the second time, the seventh house was once again triggered. Transiting Neptune, ruler of this empty house of marriage, formed a trine to the Midheaven. It is also interesting to note that Neptune rules the film industry and they collaborated in the film "Swept away" two years later. Transiting Jupiter traveling through her tenth house and forming a conjunction with the Midheaven, is further testimony of a change of status and parenthood, as she once again became a wife and now a mother of two.

The next empty house is the eighth house of sexuality ruled by Mars. Mars is found in the ninth house of exploration and religion. Madonna has frequently incorporated religion in her then controversial music videos. In October 1992, she published a scandalous book filled with her poetry, thoughts and nude photographs, titled *Sex*. At this time progressed Mercury and Venus formed a conjunction with Madonna's first house Moon, stressing the need to further express herself in a creative and literary manner. Transiting Uranus, planet of originality, shock value and rebelliousness, also formed a trine with Mars, representing sex, action and physical desires. It is interesting to note that Mars is found in her ninth house of exploration and publishing.

Mercury is her chart ruler as well as that of the Midheaven. This important planet forms a conjunction with the Moon, Pluto and the Ascendant, revealing Madonna's tremendous need to express herself through her individuality, career, and reputation. These aspects strongly demonstrate professional ambition to the extent of becoming a self-made success.

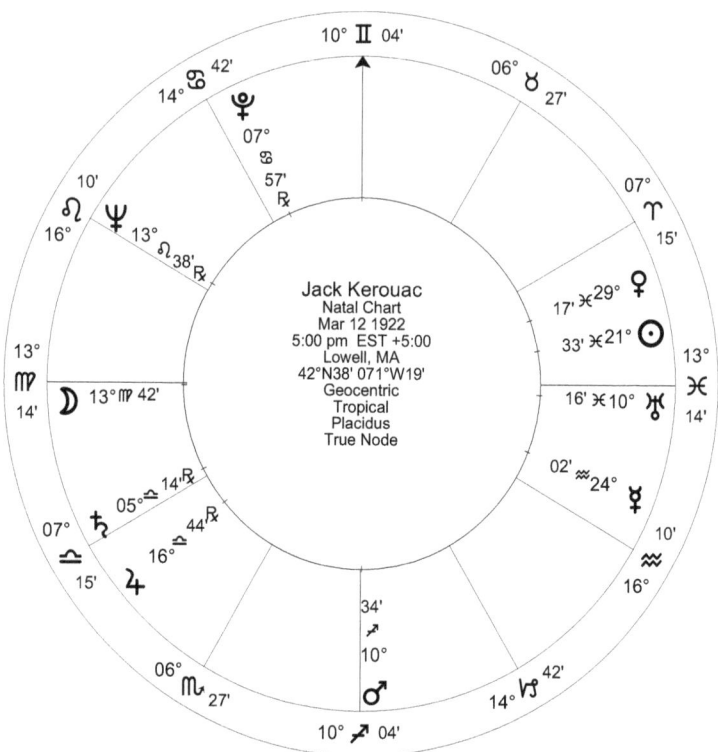

Kerouac: March 12, 1922, 5:00 a.m., Lowell, Massachusetts
Source: The Canadian Astrology Collection *by John McKay-Clements*

Jack Kerouac

As a writer, we are interested in his third house. Pluto rules this empty house revealing a highly creative, penetrating and resourceful mind. Pluto is positioned in the tenth house of career and reputation. This is indicative of a profession largely influenced or linked to matters related communications, such as public speaking or writing. It is important with this placing for the career to provide an intellectual outlet or require mental creativity. Pluto, ruler of the empty third house, also forms a sextile with the ascendant further indicating the need to project the individuality and personality through communicative or writing skills.

The third house of siblings when ruled by Pluto can bring the death of a brother or sister. Pluto is afflicted by a square with Saturn, planet of losses and ending. When Kerouac was four years old, his older brother died of rheumatic fever tremendously affecting him throughout his life. At this time progressed Moon was traveling through his first house where Saturn is located, thus activating the natal square between Saturn and Pluto.

The third house is also the sign of automobile trips and the tenth house can bring fame and honors. Kerouac was most famous for his celebrated novel that he wrote titled *On The Road*, a poignant story of friendship and trips across America.

The eighth house of death is also empty. Mars is the ruler and forms a conjunction with the fourth house cusp representing the home and family. Kerouac died in his home in Florida on October 21, 1969 at the age of 47 due to an alcohol-related disease.

Oprah Winfrey

Oprah's first house is empty and is ruled by Jupiter, found in the sixth house. Her personality is able to motivate and raise the morale of others, particularly through her work. She is happiest when at work and performing services for others, such as speaking about female empowerment. The financial outlook is excellent as Jupiter forms a trine with the Sun, Mercury and Venus in the second house of earning potential. Venus also rules her tenth house indicating much wealth gained through the career, status and reputation. She is one of America's wealthiest women. With Libra on the Midheaven, she naturally selected a profession involving interaction with the public as ruled by this sign. Jupiter in the sixth often indicates a battle with the weight.

The next empty house is the third and is ruled by Neptune. Oprah's thoughts and manner of communication are largely influenced by sincerity and compassion, qualities of Neptune. She is highly sentimental and can be easily affected by the environment and the suffering of others. Neptune is found in the tenth house and

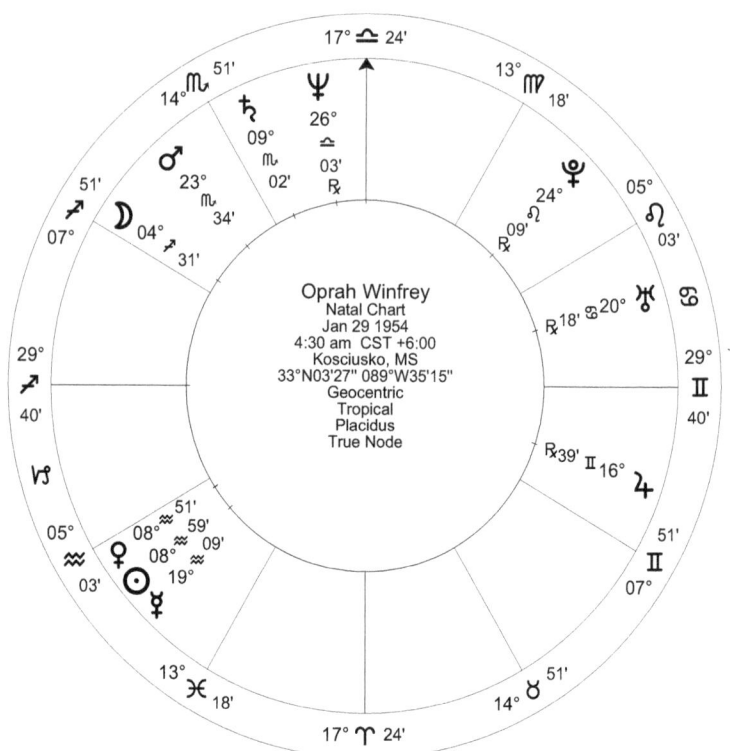

Winfrey: Jan. 29, 1954, 4:30 a.m., Kosciusko, Mississippi
Source: Lois Rodden's AstroDatabank

forms a conjunction with the Midheaven. This indicates that she can make a career out of her communicative skills of her third house. In September 1986, her self-titled talk show debuted on American television while progressed Mercury formed a trine with Saturn in the tenth. This is indicative of professional achievement and change in status. At the time of the show's debut, transiting Jupiter, planet of opportunities, luck as well as her chart ruler, formed a trine with Uranus, the planet ruling television. Twenty years later, her TV show is still hugely successful.

Oprah has no children as suggested by an empty fifth house. Venus rules this house and forms a delicate square aspect to Saturn. Venus also rules the tenth house of professional ambitions indicating that the career is chosen over motherhood.

The ninth house of publishing is also empty. It is ruled by Mercury and placed in the second house of finances. This placing indicates that earning potential can be expressed and wealth can be gained through the publishing industry. Mercury rules magazines and literature and in April 2000, she launched her own magazine, *O*. It was at this time that Mercury was triggered by a conjunction with transiting Uranus, bringing opportunities for expressing one's unique individuality. Transiting Uranus also formed a trine with Jupiter, her chart ruler and that of her empty ascendant. This brought good fortune and worthwhile opportunities for creative expression. As Jupiter is found in the sixth house, these opportunities are work-related or service-oriented.

Oprah's twelfth house is empty and also ruled by Jupiter as Sagittarius rules her twelfth and first houses. The twelfth house rules charities and related organizations and the sixth house, were Jupiter is found, indicates that work of this nature is of special interest. This placing indicates a strong need to serve, heal and guide others less fortunate. Oprah currently runs highly successful empowerment tours and seminars throughout America.

Gilles Villeneuve

Champion race car driver Gilles Villeneuve has an empty third house. This house represents road travel, vehicles and driving. As Pisces is found here, Neptune becomes the ruler. Neptune forms a conjunction with Mars bringing a tendency towards escaping through recklessness and risk-taking. This is emphasized, as Aries lies intercepted in the third house and Mars becomes the secondary or co-ruler of this empty house. Mars, planet of energy and action forms a square with Uranus, planet of sudden events and catastrophes and both these planets represent accidents, particularly when involved in a square or opposition.

Villeneuve was known for his all or nothing approach. His rep-

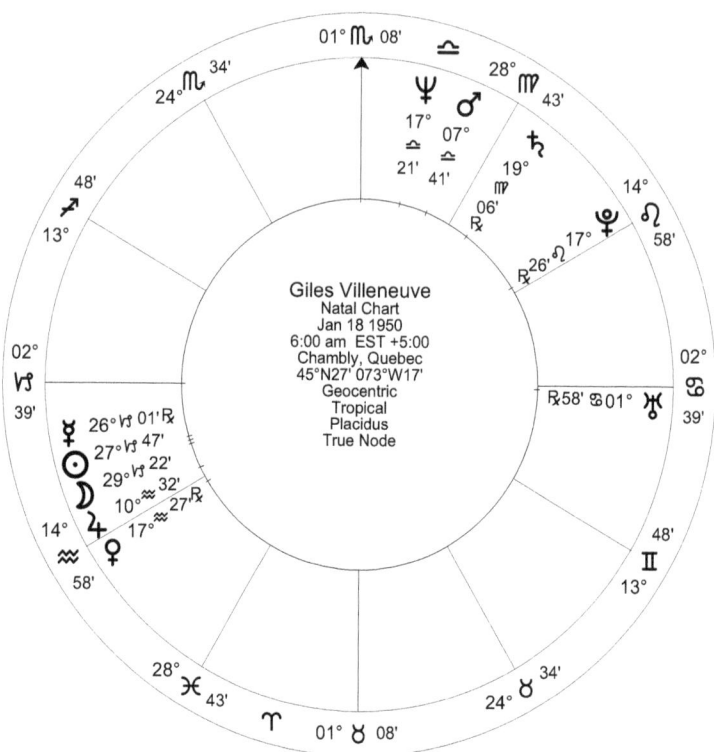

Villeneuve: Jan. 18, 1950, 6:00 a.m., Chambly, Quebec
Source: The Canadian Astrology Collection *by John McKay-Clements*

utation was that of a highly admired daredevil. It is interesting to note that his son Jacques (born April 9, 1971) follows in this father's footsteps as a race car driver. Both father and son share the dangerous Mars square Uranus aspect placed in strong cardinal signs increasing impulsiveness.

Gilles Villeneuve scored his first career win in 1978 at the Grand Prix held in Montreal, Canada. Progressed Jupiter then formed an exact conjunction with Venus, the ruler of his empty fifth house. Jupiter also formed a trine with Neptune, ruler of the third house of vehicles and driving, triggering the successful victory. The fifth house rules over racing and interestingly enough,

Villeneuve's is empty. Venus is the ruler of this house and is found in the second house. This increases the potential for wealth through such activities as racing or road travel.

Villeneuve's tenth house of fate and career is empty. Pluto, the planet of death, rules this house and is found in the eighth house of death. This strongly indicates that the end of life will be highly publicized and linked to the career. His fate was sealed and Villeneuve died in a car crash at the Belgium Grand Prix, May 8, 1982. At this time, his chart ruler Saturn, representing endings, formed a conjunction with Neptune, bringing confusion and loss of control, to the area where Neptune rules, the empty third house of vehicles and driving.

Pope John Paul II

The first house of Pope John Paul II is empty. Libra placed here on the Ascendant brings a social and diplomatic nature. Peace, justice and harmony is essential to his well-being and this is projected to others. Venus is the ruler of his chart and of this empty house. As a "man of peace" he was able to project this quality onto others as Venus is placed in the seventh house.

His second house of finances is empty revealing a lack of motivation or desire for material wealth. Pluto is the ruler of this house and is found in the ninth house. Religion, philosophy and spirituality, as ruled by the ninth house, can bring a sense of self worth as indicated by the second house of values. In other words, the gains sought and desired are spiritual and moral as opposed to financial and material. The ninth house also rules publishing, and in 1994, he was named "Man of the Year" by *Time* magazine. At that time, the progressed Sun, bringing recognition, formed a conjunction with Neptune in the tenth house of status and achievements.

On October 16, 1978, he was elected and became the first non-Italian pope in over four centuries. At this time progressed Mercury, ruler of his empty eleventh house of social issues and humanitarianism, formed a conjunction with Jupiter in the tenth

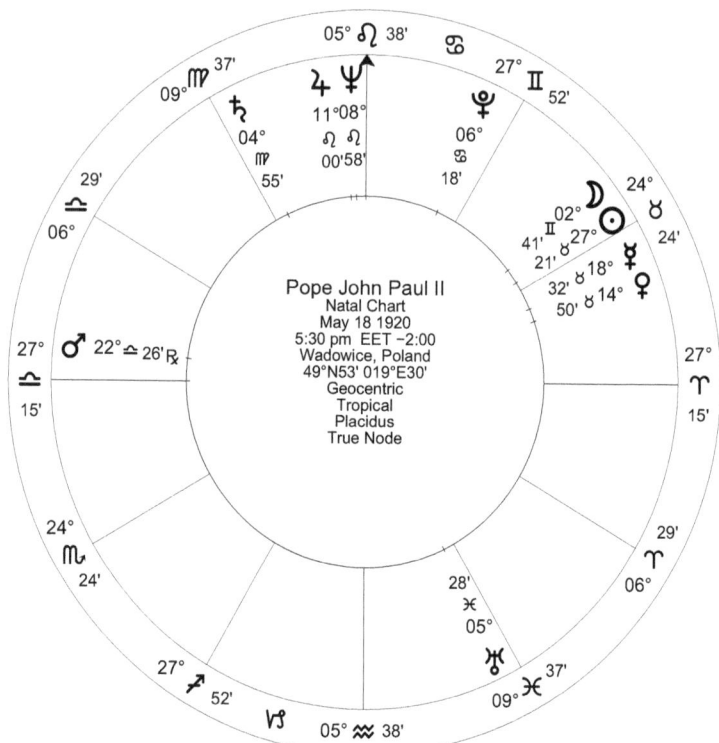

John Paul II: May 18, 1920, 5:30 p.m., Wadowice, Poland
Source: Lois Rodden's AstroDatabank

house of career, status and achievements. Transiting Jupiter, bringing opportunities and rewards, formed a conjunction with the Midheaven, Neptune and Jupiter, all in the tenth house of aspirations, culminations and accomplishments.

His sixth house of work, duty and service is also empty. Mars rules this house and is found in the twelfth house of privacy, healing, sacrifice and compassion. Work in seclusion or behind the scenes is evident, such as in places of confinement or organizations involved in secrecy. This is highly indicative of work related to the spiritual healing of others. Mars is strongly placed in this chart as it also forms a conjunction with the Ascendant.

His third house of communications is also empty. Sagittarius ruling this house brings an optimistic and philosophical intellect. This reveals ability to master foreign languages as Pope John Paul II was fluent in eight languages. Jupiter rules this house and is found in the tenth house in conjunction with the Midheaven and Neptune. This is an excellent placing for a religious or spiritual leader. A planet in conjunction with the Midheaven denotes the type of career attracted. This aspect is indicative and conducive to a profession in seclusion that can involve sacrifice or servitude. A few of the careers indicated by this conjunction are associated with religion, the church, healing, spirituality and mysticism. In *The Rulership Book* by Rex E. Bills, he states that Neptune rules Catholicism and Jupiter represents religion and religious leaders. These two planets in conjunction to the Midheaven clearly indicate his life's work and purpose.

His eleventh house of humanitarian and social interests is empty. Mercury rules this house and is found in the seventh. This is the planet of speech and communications and when found in the seventh house of the public and forming a conjunction with compassionate and social Venus, ability to touch others through words in a humanitarian manner is evident. In his public appearances, Pope John Paul II was able to convey a message of hope, wisdom, love and universal peace.

www.ingramcontent.com/pod-product-compliance
Ingram Content Group UK Ltd.
Pitfield, Milton Keynes, MK11 3LW, UK
UKHW041422180426
11947UKWH00007B/242